Y0-BCM-302

A FRAGMENT OF AUTOBIOGRAPHY

Books by John Gunther

A FRAGMENT OF AUTOBIOGRAPHY
The Fun of Writing the Inside Books

INSIDE EUROPE TODAY

TAKEN AT THE FLOOD

INSIDE RUSSIA TODAY

INSIDE AFRICA

INSIDE U.S.A.

INSIDE LATIN AMERICA

INSIDE ASIA

INSIDE EUROPE

THE RIDDLE OF MACARTHUR

EISENHOWER

ROOSEVELT IN RETROSPECT

BEHIND THE CURTAIN

DEATH BE NOT PROUD

D DAY

THE TROUBLED MIDNIGHT

DAYS TO REMEMBER
(with Bernard Quint)

MEET NORTH AFRICA

MEET SOUTH AFRICA

MEET THE CONGO

ALEXANDER THE GREAT

JULIUS CAESAR

THE GOLDEN FLEECE

George Platt Lynes

The author after *Inside Asia*

David Douglas Duncan

Twenty-five years later

JOHN GUNTHER

A FRAGMENT OF AUTOBIOGRAPHY

The Fun of Writing the Inside *Books*

HARPER & ROW, PUBLISHERS
NEW YORK AND EVANSTON

FIRST EDITION

G-M

Two excerpts from this book were first published in Harper's Magazine, *March and April, 1961.*

Library of Congress catalog card number: 62-16423

WITH LOVE TO BILLI-O

Contents

Preface, ix

I. *A Springboard in Vienna,* 1

II. *Slightly Tidier,* 24

III. *Insidoosa,* 41

IV. *Personal Invasion of Two More Continents,* 69

V. *Inside the Insides,* 96

Appendix, 114

Preface

In 1955 my good friend John Fischer, editor of *Harper's Magazine,* suggested that I write an article about how I came to write the Inside books. I was pleased and flattered, and agreed to do so. I said that nothing in the world would delight me more than to indulge myself with such an article, on the understanding, of course, that it would be brief. I said that I would apply myself to the matter immediately. Five years passed. Mr. Fischer was patient, and telephoned me once a year or so, asking how the article was getting on. I replied that I would turn it out at once. In the autumn of 1960 I suddenly found myself with a weekend free. I decided to write Mr. Fischer's article. Two months later I rose from my desk, and the job was done. It had become two articles, and these were duly published in *Harper's* in March and April, 1961, under the titles, "Exhilarated, Worn Out, Desperate, and Wildly Happy" and "An Exercise in Self-Education." Mr. Fischer was satisfied and that, I thought, was the end of the matter.

But he did suggest, somewhat vaguely, that I might someday expand what I had written into a short book. I paid scant attention to this. At roughly the same time, however, I became engaged in writing a series of bibliographical memoranda for the University of Chicago, where I was depositing my manuscripts and other personal papers. The idea then occurred to me that these, together with the *Harper's* articles, might well become the basis for a small book—a limited journey into autobiography—if I should start altogether from scratch and write it all afresh. This is what is before the reader now. It is approximately four times longer than what originally appeared in *Harper's*.

J. G.

New York City
June, 1962

A FRAGMENT OF AUTOBIOGRAPHY

CHAPTER I

A Springboard in Vienna

A GOOD MANY PEOPLE have, as a matter of fact, asked me at one time or other how I wrote the Inside books—planned the trips, worked out the logistics, assembled the material, and did the actual writing. Once, a few days after *Inside U.S.A.* was published in 1947, all 505,000 words of it, Gardner Cowles of *Look* wanted to know how much of a "staff" I had, and the late Albert D. Lasker asked the same question a little later. I was astonished, and replied that, of course, I had had no staff at all. I have always done my own leg work, as every reporter should, and have never even had a researcher. Many people have helped me profoundly in several ways, but all the Inside books are one-man jobs. I even do all the brutal, dirty business of last-ditch checking myself, which may be one reason why I sometimes feel my age, although it has been a conviction of mine for a long time that age has little to do with years.

First let me sketch briefly the history of each book, and later I will go into details of the techniques involved, if "techniques" is not too elaborate a word. I don't want to sound self-important, but I suppose I should mention at the beginning that the Inside books are all still in print and still sell steadily, which is the more remarkable in that much of the material they include is, of course, dated, and three of the seven go back twenty years or more.

I wrote the original *Inside Europe* in 1935, more than a quarter of a century ago. The calendar says this; I'm not sure I really believe it. The seven have been translated into a total of twenty-one foreign languages, and although nobody could know their imperfections better than I do, they have become, as it were, "standard" works. Chapters from them have appeared in some sixty textbooks and anthologies, and the impact of several has been substantial not merely in the United States but abroad. None has ever done as well as single books by friends of mine, for instance Bill Shirer's triumphant *Rise and Fall of the Third Reich,* but their record, considered as a group, is quite good.

As a matter of fact, although many facts and figures in the early Insides are dated, the books as a whole, viewed in an over-all way, are not. I was attempting to make a bridge between history and the news, and most of the background material which the books contain still holds up. The best proof of this, aside from the fact that all are still in print, is that thousands of visitors to this country still use *Inside U.S.A.*, for example, as a guidebook, although it was never intended to be such. Similarly, many people going to Africa still find *Inside Africa* useful, although it was published in 1955 and Africa has changed beyond belief since then. But the book continues to hold a certain value, if only because no other has come along to replace it. The same thing is true of *Inside Russia Today,* some chapters of which still read as if they had been written this morning.

Friends flatter me by saying, in explanation of all this, that the Inside books filled—and still fill—a need, which is the basis of the survival of most commodities. Nobody else has ever attempted to do quite the kind of book, embracing whole continents, which I did. I do not know why. The pattern was there for anybody to pick up. Anyway, they are all still alive and, in their own way, are a unique phenomenon in the view of many people. So I hope that I may be excused for this attempt to put part of the record down.

II

Each Inside book was a scramble against time—in several cases against harassing circumstances as well—and each was the product of somewhat disorderly procedures, although the key to everything in the kind of work I try to do is, or should be, organization. Journalism, like history, is certainly not an exact science.

The origins of *Inside Europe* are the following: In the early 1930's I was Vienna correspondent of the Chicago *Daily News,* an admirable newspaper, with Central Europe and the Balkans as my territory. I stretched all the way from the Adriatic to the Golden Horn, and was responsible for nine countries (Austria, Czechoslovakia, Hungary, Yugoslavia, Albania, Rumania, Bulgaria, Greece and Turkey), all of which I attempted to visit intermittently. We had wings on our heels in those dulcet days, even if the Orient Express was slow.

I took my job seriously, although the swarms of friends and visitors who encountered me in the coffee houses night after night might not have thought so. If I missed a story by cable I would try to dress it up with a new "lead" and send it by mail. My hope was that, if a Chicago reader followed our foreign news page carefully, he would be reasonably well informed about my galaxy of countries. I was interested in the *record.* Then, for a variety of reasons, one of which was certainly the need to earn more money, I began writing for various magazines. *Vanity Fair,* the *Nation,* the *New Republic,* the *Woman's Home Companion,* the *Saturday Evening Post,* even *Foreign Affairs,* printed articles of mine, and I came to be known in a small way as a youngster with an eye for Central Europe and its problems—everything from dynastic rivalries in Rumania to the Hapsburg succession, from Comitadji violence in Macedonia to what was going on in Prague. All this work, as well as work for the *News* itself, helped me considerably when it came time to write *Inside Europe* later.

Another factor demands a paragraph of flashback. Before being assigned to a post of my own in Vienna (1930), I spent several years as second-man in the *News* bureaus in London and Paris, under Hal O'Flaherty and Paul Scott Mowrer. As the junior man on the staff I filled in too for our other bureau chiefs (Berlin, Rome, Geneva, Moscow) when they went home on leave. Moreover, I was at hand to cover emergencies elsewhere—everything from a political crisis in Spain to riots in Israel, then known as Palestine. This gave me varied experience. My boss in Paris, Paul Scott Mowrer, a keenly sensitive and percipient man, saw presently that I was not much good at spot news. Indeed, I have scarcely ever had a scoop in my life, and it seemed to me abysmally silly, then as now, to break a neck trying to beat the opposition by a few seconds on a story, although I knew why this was necessary. Paul realized that my talents, if any, lay elsewhere. It seems that I had a knack for being readable about situations and people, and I was nimble with feature stories. I had little basic interest in politics, a fault which besets me to this day, but I was ravenously interested in human beings. So, when I was not substituting for our senior men in a big capital or covering an emergency, Paul would send me to some country or other to prowl around for a week or two and write my impressions. The stories that resulted always had a hard news basis—what was happening in the given country, how, and why—but I flavored my text with as much "human interest" material as possible. On such missions I worked in Sweden, Albania, Egypt, Syria, Spain, Poland, and Turkey. Hence, by the time I was assigned to a bureau of my own, Vienna, I had picked up dust from almost every European country. My knowledge was, heaven knows, spotty, but I had covered a lot of ground.

(Incredibly enough, some of those early mail stories still arouse interest by specialists. I received a letter in March, 1962, from a Yugoslav friend asking if I could dig out for him the articles I had written about Macedonia in December, 1928.)

The 1930's were the bubbling, blazing days of American foreign correspondence in Europe. This was before journalism became institutionalized. Not a single American embassy had a press or cultural affairs officer. We correspondents were strictly on our own. Naturally, we cultivated friendships with American officials and diplomats, as well as those of other countries, but not quite in the manner of today. We did not think of ourselves as being instruments of a national policy. We avoided official handouts. We were scavengers, buzzards, out to get the news, no matter whose wings got clipped. We all had strong personal points of view, which we did not bother to dissemble. My own paper had a magnificent staff—Paul Mowrer in Paris, his brother Edgar in Berlin, William H. Stoneman in Rome, Negley Farson in London, Junius B. Wood in Moscow. On other papers were other giants. Various capitals became personified by the leading correspondents in each. Walter Duranty *was* Moscow; Raymond Swing *was* London; Jay Allen *was* Madrid; H. R. Knickerbocker and Dorothy Thompson *were* Berlin.

Most of us traveled steadily, met constantly, exchanged information, caroused, took in each other's washing, and, even when most fiercely competitive, were devoted friends.

I lived in Vienna from 1930 to 1935. It is something extraordinary to relate, but I performed the miracle of *not* learning enough German to be able to speak it decently after almost five years of residence in a German-speaking country. Nor did I ever learn good French. There can be no excuse for this, but the bent of my mind lay elsewhere.

In 1931 appeared *Washington Merry-Go-Round,* by Drew Pearson and Robert Allen. It was a signal success, and several publishers conceived the idea of commissioning a similar book on Europe. Out of the blue one day I got a letter from Long & Smith, a house now defunct, inviting me to contribute to an anonymous book on Europe to be called "Not to Be Repeated," on the Merry-Go-Round model. Somebody was to do France, somebody England, and so on, and I was asked to write Austria and the Balkans. The cash advance offered was small, $150 if my memory is right, but, like all of us, I was hard up; besides, the idea was challenging, and I accepted. I wrote five chapters and in due course the book was published. Instantly it died the death. I never met anybody who ever heard of it.

Meantime Cass Canfield of Harper & Brothers had an idea for the same kind of book, but on a more comprehensive, serious level. So did Frances Gunther. She was very much part of this whole process. Canfield, who became my staff of life for twenty-five years and more, asked me to do the job for him, tackling the whole continent. I replied that I didn't know enough, and that the only person in the world who did and who could write it was my friend and colleague, the late H. R. Knickerbocker. Canfield approached Knickerbocker, who replied promptly that he did not want to do it and that the only person in the world who could was none other than his friend Gunther. So Cass came back to me.

But I continued to say no. In those days I was more interested in fiction than in journalism and my dreams were tied up in a long novel about Vienna that I hoped to write. In the autumn of 1934 I returned home on leave, and met Canfield in New York, together with Bernice Baumgarten of Brandt & Brandt, my agents. I persisted in saying no to the project and finally Miss Baumgarten asked me what, if any, financial advance would induce me to change my mind. To cut the whole matter off I named the largest sum I had ever heard of —$5,000. To my consternation Miss Baumgarten said that she could get this, and she approached Canfield and several other publishers. Five thousand dollars was a lot of money in those days, as it still is, even to a house like Harper's, but in the end the sum was made up. Harper's itself agreed to contribute $3,000, Hamish Hamilton (who had recently started publishing in London) $1,000, and *Harper's Magazine* $1,000 in payment for three articles to be derived from the book. It was carefully pointed out to me, moreover, that this rate of pay, $333.33 per article, was much more than the magazine was accustomed to paying at the time. (The three articles turned out to be the three chief personality chapters in the book—Hitler, Mussolini, and Stalin.) But I still could not quite nerve myself to agree to take on such a difficult and ambitious project, went to

Chicago, and did not return to New York until a month or two later. It is my curse, or blessing, that I have never been able to take myself altogether seriously as a writer.

So I continued to defy all attempts to make me put my name to an actual contract, and early in the morning of the day that I was to sail back to my Vienna post, just before Christmas, 1934, Canfield marched into the Hotel Chatham before I was out of bed and announced that he would sit in the room all day if necessary, so that I would miss the boat, if I did not sign up. Finally I agreed, although I did not actually put my name to paper until months later. Now, of course, I wake up every once in a while wondering what on earth my life would have been like if Canfield, so quietly tenacious and persuasive, had not made his final artful approach that wintry morning so long ago.

After returning to Vienna I got to work. I did not anticipate much difficulty. I wrote the Rumanian chapter first. This was to be a pacemaker; I wanted to feel myself out. It went like a dream. I was basking in the relative contentment, even torpor, of Vienna; my *News* job did not, to be frank, take a full twenty-five hours a day. Then in April, 1935, I was suddenly transferred by the Chicago *Daily News* from Vienna to London. London! This was, needless to say, a very long jump: Vienna was small-time; London was big. I had to establish relationships, since these are the basis of journalism. I had to learn my way about, although I knew London fairly well. I had, if possible, to get "in." I was in charge of our most important European bureau, and I was singlehanded. Moreover, crisis followed crisis that agitated year; news poured out; we had everything to deal with from the Ethiopian War to a general election. This was no longer Vienna; I had to work at my job six days a week, eight or ten hours a day.

Hence the book for Harper's, to which I was now irrevocably committed, had to be written in what might euphemistically be called spare time—also in a hurry; the material was highly perishable. Night after night and all day on Sundays I trudged from our apartment on Gower Street to the *News* office in Bush House, crushed by pressure, exhilarated, worn out, desperate, and wildly happy. Looking back today, I still don't know how I managed to do a moderately acceptable job as a news correspondent during the day with enough energy for a book at night. But, after all, I was only thirty-three.

In order to do a conscientious book I had, of course, to freshen up on Europe as a whole. From Vienna that would have been easy. I could always contrive weekend trips to any place within reason. But London kept me cemented firmly to a desk. Luckily I had a vacation due—three precious weeks. So (it sounds like lunacy now) I contrived to visit Paris, Rome, Berlin, and Moscow in those three weeks. Meantime colleagues helped me, Knickerbocker most of all. He knew more about Hitler, Stalin, and Mussolini than any other newspaperman in Europe, and on three successive long afternoons in London he valiantly, brilliantly emptied himself of these subjects for my benefit. Of course I used other sources too. Then Jay Allen gave me memoranda on Spain, Ralph Forte on Italy, Morris Gilbert on France, M. W. Fodor on the Balkans. At one lunch in London the late Stephan Litauer, the best-known Polish journalist of the day, almost literally talked my Pilsudski chapter to me in three hours.

What I sought, among much else, was material for human rather than purely political portraits. I drew up a list of questions to ask about my major characters:

Attitude to religion
Attitude to sex
Attitude to fame
Attitude to money
Motivations; great decisions
Pet hates; pet likes
Ambition
What are his fundamental sources of *power*
Chief intellectual qualities
Chief moral qualities, if any
Defects
What does he believe in most
Relaxations, hobbies
Daily routine; method of work
Family background
Stresses in childhood; influences in youth
Chief turning points in career
Interest in books, music, art, if any
Health and physical condition
Friends; those closest to him, attitude to subordinates
Nicknames
Tastes in food and drink
Anecdotes
What has been his contribution
Danger of assassination; how protected
Who will succeed him

In London and elsewhere I posed these questions in regard to men all the way from Kemal Ataturk to Masaryk, from Laval to Stanley Baldwin. I have followed the same procedure ever since, and my list of questions has changed little.

To proceed, a great many people gave me information. Everybody likes gossip and I was treating gossip, as one British lady put it, "in the grand manner." Newsmen were delighted to have a colleague write things that, for various reasons, they themselves had to sit on. But I must also emphasize that the conception and design of my book were totally my own and did not vary much from the structure I had worked out for it at the beginning, to the effect that I would peg my material to the leading personalities, hanging political background on them. Also from the very beginning I wanted to stress what really made power in each country—who or what *ran* it. Then the design grew with the writing. I do not, however, think that I got the idea of starting with Germany and ending with Russia until I was half done. My memory now is that my first impulse was to begin with England, which would have been the conventional approach. How glad I am now that I had the journalistic savvy to grab on to Hitler and make him the lead!

Somehow—I still don't know how—I finished the actual writing in seven months and copies of the manuscript went to New York and to Hamish Hamilton, the agile young Scot who was my London publisher. Until the extreme last moment there had to be revisions because we wanted the book to be up to date, above all. Sir Samuel Hoare resigned from the British government (and was replaced by Mr. Eden) between galley proofs and page proofs, and other events which demanded inclusion occurred actually after page proofs had been closed. Well, we opened them again. Also, Hamilton had the script checked for libel by no fewer than three lawyers, none of whom knew that the others were reading it. This meant more revision. At the end I myself correlated tediously the American and British copies of the manuscript; I still recall the memorandum I typed out, because doing it took all night in the Bush House office; I think this was the first time I had ever stayed up all night on a job and a startled secretary found me, bent over the desk like a lobster claw, in the same crazed, concentrated position at 9:30 in the morning that I had been in when she left the night before. It was all a wonderful mad rush and both Canfield and Hamilton performed mechanical prodigies in manufacturing the book promptly. We closed proofs finally just before Christmas and yet the book came out in February, 1936. Of course, since that date it has been revised, reset, and republished several times. By accident I invented what has subsequently become known as "book journalism"; a book became a kind of periodical. More on this below.

III

Until almost the last moment we had no title. Rather, we had twenty titles. These ranged from "The New Europe" to "The Age of the Dictators." I think that, as the last chapter was being written, the book was called "Men Over Europe"—or something even more unsatisfactory. The question of title tortured me. I was obsessed. In November I had to take time out to cover the British election, and I visited various constituencies, including Seaham Harbour where Ramsay MacDonald was fighting for his political life, but I could think of nothing but my book. On a day wet with brown clinging fog I found myself in Ebbw Vale in the Welsh coal fields with the late Aneurin Bevan. He brought me up to date on what was going on and drove me over roads covered with icy slime to Cardiff, where I boarded the train for London. I don't think I've ever been so damp and cold in my life. I had a Scotch or two in the restaurant car, gazing through smearily misted windows at a procession of seemingly identical brick villages with curving streets. I kept saying to myself, "I must find a title, I *must* find a title!" Abstract thought is foreign to my nature, but I sought to reason the matter out. What was my book about? It was about Europe. What kind of view of Europe did it give? Well, it tried to tell the true story of the dictators who were dominating our lives, threatening our institutions, from a particular point of view—an intimate view, an inside view. Suddenly I had it. An Insider's Europe. . . . Looking at Europe from the Inside. . . . Inside Europe! I was terrified that I might forget this before reaching London, and scribbled the words in the margin of a copy of the London *Times,* while munching a cold, fatty lump of mutton. I reached London, called Hamilton, and, in a frenzy of excitement, tried "Inside Europe" on him. He liked it instantly and cabled Canfield, who liked it too. So our book had a title at last.

Heaven knows I didn't invent the word "inside" and it had already been used in novels like *The Inside of the Cup,* by the other Winston Churchill. Later I learned that *Variety,* a magazine which I am not sure I had ever seen as of that day, ran a column called "Inside Stuff." But this wasn't my field and for many years I held comfortably to the view that the word "inside" had never been used before as I was using it. Then, a decade later, I found out to my astonishment that Herbert Bayard Swope had written a report on Germany during the First World War called "Inside the German Empire." Mr. Swope himself mentioned this to me years later, and chided me gently. Even so, it can be fairly stated that the Inside title, as made popular by me, was my own invention. Of course, I am so sick of it now that I wince when I hear it, but it has rendered me stout service. Other writers have imitated it hundreds of times—thousands. There are at least twenty books called Inside or Outside something or other, among them

Inside the Whale, by George Orwell, a book about prisons called simply *Inside,* by Helen Bryan, *Inside Marriage, Inside Benchley, Inside the Atom,* and even *Inside Inside,* an anthology sponsored by the Overseas Press Club. Syngman Rhee, the Korean dictator now deposed, once wrote a book called *Japan Inside Out.*

As to magazine and newspaper stories, these exist almost without number. Whenever an editor cannot think of another title he simply tacks the word "inside" on his subject. Examples run from "Inside the Garden of Eden" to "Inside Joe DiMaggio's Batting" and even "Inside Outer Space."

In one year, 1952, I came across no fewer than seventy-two uses of Inside in newspapers and magazines. Some sprightly items, in this and other years, were:

"Inside Our Schools via Television"

"Inside Wonderland" (an article on Liechtenstein)

"Inside Retailing" (a handout from a fashion house)

"Inside Story of an Outsider"

"Inside Passage"

"Inside the Rock" (Alcatraz)

"Inside the Lunar Base" (an article in *Look*)

"Inside Interior" (a house organ of the Department of the Interior, Washington)

"Inside Los Angeles' Chinatown" (a privately printed brochure)

"Inside a Moslem Arabian Nights' Palace"

"Inside Tin Pan Alley"

"Inside Walter Winchell"

"Inside Today" (a weather report in a newspaper)

"Inside Summer" (an article in *Vogue*)

"Inside the Sour Mash Bourbon Business"

There have been several "Inside Red Chinas," and, bless me, even an "Inside Russia Today."

Actually, the Inside title as used by me was truly

applicable to only one of my books, the first one, *Inside Europe*. After that I was not so much inside looking out as outside looking in. One of the reasons that I dislike the title nowadays is that, as used by many other writers, it has come to connote vulgarity and sensationalism, as well as false intimacy, which, if I do say so myself, I have always sought to avoid, although I like gossip as much as the next man. However, the title has been of substantial aid to me because it has given me an identification, a kind of trademark, so that my series of books seems to have a structural unity, a continuing design. Besides it has saved me from the considerable nuisance of finding a new title for each new work.

I suppose I should add a word about the jokes. Such appalling jokes! Few days go by, even now, that I am not asked by somebody when more of my insides are coming out or when I am going to write "Inside Gunther." I don't think a week has passed in twenty years, that, arriving at a large gathering, I have not been greeted by somebody with the coy question, "And what are you *inside* of now, Mr. Gunther?" and, visiting a city, I have heard the arch phrase, "Ah, you are *inside* Buffalo now" or "Now you can write an article about being *inside* the Hotel Flamingo" at least ten thousand times.

IV

An interviewer once asked me what was the most rewarding single moment associated with the Inside books. One certainly occurred on Gower Street the day *Inside Europe* was published in England in February, 1936. Frances Gunther picked up the *Daily Telegraph* and a peculiar expression came over her face, both luminous and cryptic. She said, "Listen to this," and began to read aloud from a review of the book by Harold Nicolson. I thought she must be making it up—joking. I could not believe that any critic, particularly Nicolson, whom I fervently admired but whom I had never met, could possibly use such terms about anything by me. One of his phrases was "I regard this book as a serious contribution to contemporary knowledge." The review went on: "Fair, intelligent, balanced and well informed . . . It will provide the intelligent reader with exactly that sort of information on current affairs which he desires to possess and which he can acquire from no other equally readable source. . . . A book which can be read as a romance. . . . I can conceive no phrase in which better to convey to readers the necessity of acquiring this book. . . . This is one of the most educative as well as one of the most exciting books which I have read for years." I blushed with excitement. I could not believe my eyes or ears.

Looking back now over the entire course I think that, on the whole, my books have been overpraised. I have been severely clobbered on occasion but in general I have had good luck with reviews and my books have not always deserved what has been said about them, though I do not mean to sound ungenerous to a multitude of friendly critics. Next to the Nicolson review, the best that I have ever had were those on *Asia* by Rodney Gilbert (in the New York *Herald Tribune Books*), who called it "the most competent one-man reportorial job ever undertaken," by John Mason Brown on *Roosevelt in Retrospect* in the *Saturday Review of Literature,* and by Alan Paton on *Africa* in the New York *Herald Tribune Books.* Bad reviews have annoyed me as they must annoy any author, but if they were fair-minded and not motivated by spite I have always tried to control my anger and to learn from them. If a critic has read a book thoroughly and has serious, well-reasoned adverse points to make, the author should take heed carefully. The experience is unpleasant, but it may turn out to be of value.

Inside Europe caught on in England at once and before the week was out Hamilton knew that he had a hit. The book became, in fact, the biggest success he had ever had as a publisher, and I have even been told that it sold more copies in England than any other work of nonfiction by an American since Mark Twain. I am sure that this must be an exaggeration. Publication came in the United States a few weeks later and here too the critical reception was good, but at the beginning the book did not sell as well as in England. British readers were closer to the subject. A month or so after publication we began to get offers for translations, and presently I found myself appearing in languages all the way from Dutch and Danish to Hungarian and Estonian. There are weird tales to be told about some of these translations. The French, I soon learned, have an insularity all their own about books. Their translation of *Inside Europe* was, for instance, a miserable little volume called *Les Pilotes de l'Europe,* which did not contain more than a third of the text of the American, British, or other foreign editions. Not till a similar experience with the French edition of *Inside Africa* many years later was I subjected to such a brutal manhandling. Oddities also occurred in connection with Spain. No Spanish edition could be published in Spain itself because of the Franco dictatorship, but after a time the book appeared in Argentina, as have all subsequent books of mine that have been translated into Spanish. Then a house in Chile printed another Spanish edition, called *Los Amos de Europa,* which was pirated. I think it was a translation of the French edition; anyway, it is brief.

The most flagrant pirates are the Chinese because,

then as now, they do not subscribe to the International Copyright Union. I did not even know that *Inside Europe* existed in Chinese until I visited China a year or two later. The ingenious Chinese published it in the form of a series of pamphlets, each dealing with a single country and each bound picturesquely with a picture of its flag on the cover—the Union Jack for England, the Swastika for Germany, and so on. These pamphlets made a debonair display in the bookstores and on newspaper stands, and I have often wondered why no publisher in some other country has ever thought of doing the same thing—legally.

Translations make very little money for the author, even if they do well. Usually the writer gets a modest advance and that is the end of the matter. The Japanese, Dutch, and Swedes are, in my experience, the most satisfying of foreign publishers to deal with—in recent years the Italians too. The Japanese in particular, in strict contrast to the Chinese, are punctiliously correct in money matters.

Used as I use it, the word "inside" apparently defies translation, and it has been fascinating to see how this problem is handled in different languages. My Spanish translators in the Argentine started out with *El Drama de Europa* and have held to this formula ever since; the Portuguese (in Rio de Janeiro, not Lisbon) used *O Drama da Europa* for many years until *Inside Russia Today* came along; this appeared as *A Rússia por Dentro.* In Dutch the same title has held straight through—*Europa in de Branding, Afrika in de Branding,* etc. In Danish I am always behind the Continent's "kulisser," which I believe means curtain, and in Swedish the term for witch's kettle makes the title. In early days, when I could not be published in Germany itself, the Germans who published me abroad used *So Sehe Ich Europa,* but since the end of the war they have tried to get closer to the title in English; e.g., *Afrika von Innen. Inside U.S.A.* came out in French as *Passport Pour les U.S.A.*; *Inside Africa* became *L'Autre Afrique.* With one book, *Inside U.S.A.,* the Italians used a straight-out translation of "inside"— *Dentro l'America*—but *Inside Russia* is *Russia Oggi.* I have no idea what the title means as translated into several other European languages like Bulgarian and Czech, nor in various Oriental languages.

Suppressions of *Inside Europe* make a little story too. No German publisher would have dared to publish it in Germany itself during the Hitler era, but anti-Hitler refugees put it out in the Netherlands in 1937. Meantime, in May, 1936, a friend in Germany sent me a copy of the following official order:

> The book Inside Europe by John Gunther, published by Hamish Hamilton, has been confiscated and withdrawn from circulation.
> B.—N.R. II.
> 2 E 164025.3.36
> Berlin 35.3.36 GESTAPO

Later, during the war, I was honored by inclusion in the select company of American writers on an official Gestapo "death list." Apparently the Nazis thought that I still lived in England and, when England was duly invaded and conquered, I was among those who were to be executed at once, if caught. There were several mentions of *Inside Europe* at the Nuremburg trials. One defendant, Dr. Wilhelm Frick, who was subsequently hanged, asked that passages from the book be put in evidence, though I do not know why.

Other countries, including several of the Fascist puppet states, followed the German example quickly. The Hungarian translation was suppressed soon after its publication in Budapest (I have a copy of it, though) and a Polish edition (I have never seen it) was, I am told, withdrawn just before it was to have reached the bookstores. Contracts were signed for a Yugoslav edition, but political pressure from the dictatorship then ruling in Belgrade forced its cancellation, and I have been told that my Yugoslav translator was actually sentenced to jail for a brief period. Efforts were made to translate the book into both Bulgarian and Turkish, but negotiations fell through before they reached the contract stage. The book was never formally forbidden in Italy but it was not translated into Italian and it was impossible to get the American or British editions in Italian bookshops.

Finally in this general field I would like to mention that, some years after original publication, *Inside Europe* came out in Braille, and filled five stout volumes.

I don't remember quite how we decided to keep *Inside Europe* alive by continually revising and republishing it. Probably the first stimulus came from Hamilton. A month after publication—in March, 1936—he asked me to write a new preface describing events that had occurred in Europe since closing proofs a few months earlier. History moved rapidly in those days, and I finished this new preface, which was brief, on the very day that Hitler marched into the Rhineland. So another new preface became necessary at once, which we inserted into the book in May. In both cases the text of the body of the book was unchanged. We even counted *letters* in each word in several passages, so that new sentences could be slipped into the new prefaces without having to reset the paragraphs.

Then began the much more elaborate process whereby I several times revised the book from top to bottom, so that it had to be totally reset and published anew. Edition followed edition. This produced a lot of bad jokes in the publishing business, such as that the book had a new "model" every year like an automobile, and could be bought on a trade-in basis, or that it ought to be put out in loose-leaf. One unseemly quip was that it should be called "The Almanach de Guntha." In blunt fact Harper's for a time offered individual purchasers a 50-cent rebate on old copies turned in for new.

The first of these completely revised and reset editions appeared in October, 1936, eight months after original publication. I eliminated some material that had already become dated, made numerous minor changes, added new sections on the Rhineland crisis and the Ethiopian War, and wrote two new chapters, one on Léon Blum, who had become Prime Minister in France, and one on Eamon de Valera. Later I wrote another dealing with the abdication of King Edward VIII, and this was duly inserted in this new edition.

Then in the summer of 1937 came a second complete revision. It was published in November, and contained new chapters on the Russian treason trials, the neutral states, and the Spanish Civil War. Events continued to pursue us implacably, and in October, 1938, I wrote two more new chapters on Munich and the Fascist Offensive. These were inserted into what was called the "Peace" Edition of the book, and, finally, after the outbreak of the war, I did a "1940 War Edition" which, once more, was revised from beginning to end, reset, and republished.

One result of all this continuing process was that *Inside Europe,* which was 180,000 words long on its first publication in 1936, grew to a length of about 265,000 words by 1940. Several peculiar bibliographical details might be mentioned. For instance, on page 248 of the first U.S. revision two or three lines of text are replaced by dots. I haven't the faintest idea why this was done but presumably Harper's did not want the page to have an empty patch when I cut some material from the previous edition. I do not know why I did not write a substitute passage. Also I have discovered, while writing this present reminiscence, that one chapter in an early American edition is paginated by letters, not numbers. No doubt this was done to avoid the expense of repaginating the whole book. I never noticed it before.

One technical point perplexed me greatly in those days, and still troubles me—namely, *how* up to date a book of journalism should be. Obviously enough, if you make something *too* up to date this is likely to have a contrary effect and will make your text out of date the more quickly. No one wants to read an almanac (except possibly me). On the other hand, it is necessary to be timely.

Despite all these changes, insertions, subtractions, revisions, deletions, and additions in *Inside Europe* from 1936 to 1940, its essential structure and point of view remained unaltered. My basic pattern—the overriding idea I had at the outset—never changed. In fact, one could almost say that Hitler and Company filled in for me the outline I had adumbrated. My book began with Hitler and said that he would certainly make a war; it ended with Stalin and said that Soviet Russia was the key to what would happen in the future.

Glancing through the book recently I found a few paragraphs which, from the point of view of style, I liked—for instance, the passage in which I said that Stalin's nerves, if he had any, must be veins in rock. But also I found myself cringing with embarrassment at the multitude of verbal infelicities it contains—youthful overuse of exclamation points, clauses separated by commas instead of semicolons, use of slang and journalese, too much quotation, slipshod paragraphing, and plain bad usage.

Why did *Inside Europe* do so well? Why, like a pebble unlodged, did it set into motion an avalanche of books by other newspaper writers, and help found a school? One reason was that it revealed much that had not been generally known before. A few correspondents and diplomats knew the truth about men like Kemal Ataturk and Pilsudski, but not the public at large. Much that is now common knowledge about everybody from Mussolini to Ramsay MacDonald had never been printed until I broke the taboo. The book was news. Then again readers seemed to feel that it had a quality of detachment, objectivity, which derived not only from my own cast of mind but from the tutelage of the Chicago *Daily News.* Once, many years later, Colonel Nasser of Egypt, whom I have never met, told a friend that what I wrote had to be taken seriously because I always gave both sides—one of the pleasantest compliments I have ever received. Finally, *Inside Europe* was among the first books to point out cogently the epochal challenge to our way of life made by the three great totalitarian dictators. Plenty of people were in those days pro-Mussolini; plenty of prominent Americans and Britons still thought that, as the phrase went, we could do business with Hitler. Most of my colleagues and I did not. Years later somebody on the London *Daily Express* said that I was the man "who put the wind up the world in 1936." This is exaggeration to the point of comedy, but I did try to write the facts.

CHAPTER II

Slightly Tidier

NEXT CAME *Inside Asia.* This derived from a process slightly tidier and more systematic. For *Inside Europe* I had had twelve years of residence in Europe to draw upon, but I had never been in Asia at all except twice for brief trips to the Middle East, and consequently I had to plan and execute a journey deliberately taken with the object of obtaining information and, out of direct experience, writing a report. My aim was to see every country in Asia, of which there were about thirty at that time; I fell short by half a dozen. This procedure —an extensive trip so that I could inspect or survey at first hand what I wanted to write about—has been basic to my working habits ever since. (Not that there is anything unusual about this, except that it requires a spacious investment in energy and time.)

Obviously *Inside Europe* had, without intent, created a pattern which could be followed by books on other continents—though I do not believe that at that time my thinking had crystallized into a definite program of charting the whole of the known political world, continent by continent. But I wrote Canfield on February 3, 1936, before my book on Europe was even published, to the effect that I would like someday to do similar books on Asia and the United States. A supplementary germ for *Asia* came from my seven-year-old son, Johnny, who, after *Inside Europe,* suggested one day that I should do "Inside the North Pole." Years later my friend Clifton Fadiman asked what I would do when I ran out of continents, and then gave his own quick answer, "Try incontinence."

I quit the Chicago *Daily News* in September, 1936, and moved back to America. I did not have $2,000 in the world. To quit a good job was a gamble. But most of the good luck I have had in my professional life has come from quitting jobs. Then, in October, 1937, accompanied by Frances Gunther, I set out for Asia. Originally the book was to be called *Inside Orient.* The trip lasted until the summer of 1938—about ten months. I wrote the book, which runs to about 250,000 words, in Westport, Connecticut, and New York City between September, 1938, and April, 1939. Actually the net writing time was only about five months. I still do not believe that this could be so; but it was. The difference between gross time and net time is accounted for by interruptions. I had to take time out for the several revisions of *Inside Europe,* for a lecture tour, and to write magazine articles with which I earned my keep. There was the sharp necessity of financing myself during the period of the undertaking. Here I must pause to explain something. A trip around the world costs money. In those days I never had a cent of expense account money from publishers or magazines, although Harper's and Hamilton always gave me a generous advance on royalties. However, the royalty advances were, as a rule, mostly spent before I left my doorstep, for the simple reason that, while a writer is on an extended trip, the normal expenditures of a family go on and money has to be allotted in advance for rent, taxes, insurance, and the like. Also initial expenses for transportation are considerable.

My own way out of this vexing dilemma was to do magazine articles as I went along—an onerous procedure. At a time when every atom of energy should have been devoted to taking in I had to give out—a process roughly equivalent to putting on the brakes suddenly while driving uphill. It takes precious time from the primary purpose of the trip, which is to obtain information. I still remember with acute anguish days I have had to spend grinding out articles when I should have been submerging myself in the atmosphere of a situation or a community. I lost a week or more in India writing about Palestine and the Middle East; I lost a week in Hong Kong writing about Malaya and Indonesia. (Years later I had to miss out on some marvelous experiences in Kenya because I had to lock myself up for a grisly period to do an article about another part of Africa which we had just visited.)

Anyway, I sounded out *Fortune,* the *Saturday Evening Post,* the North American Newspaper Alliance, and other magazines and agencies before we left New York for Asia. I believe that I wrote at least nine long articles during the trip, including a newspaper series on the Sino-Japanese War as seen from Hankow; also, I did several spot news interviews for NANA, by cable, including one with Generalissimo Chiang Kai-shek. Among the articles were several from India and Japan which appeared in the *Nation,* long pieces about Singapore, the Indian Princes, and the Japanese Army in Manchuria for the *Saturday Evening Post,* and several—one was called "Kings in the Middle East"—which I was never able to sell anywhere. And there was "Partition in Palestine" for *Harper's Magazine* and still another, about Siam, which appeared in *Foreign Affairs.*

To an extent this process had a compensating feature, in that I had a backlog of material already written when it came time to do the book. But it is my experience that any journalism done during a trip has to be completely rewritten for book purposes. No book that is simply a compilation of newspaper or magazine articles ever turns out to be a book. Scissors and paste are not enough. This is a law. Magazine writing and book writing are totally different. Tone and structure in a book should be altogether different. For instance, in a newspaper story the lead, or main point, belongs on top; in a chapter of a book it may be more effective at the end. Even paragraphing should be different. Most writers trained on newspapers write short paragraphs because these suit a narrow column of type. But paragraphs in a book should, to my mind, be long. I can almost always tell a nonbook from a book at first glance, because the paragraphing in the former is likely to be very short.

Inside Asia marked the beginning of a long, fruitful association with *Reader's Digest.* As soon as I returned to the United States the late Carl Brandt, my agent and close friend, sent me out to Pleasantville to see De Witt and Lila Wallace for one of the most rewarding afternoons of my life. They agreed to pick up the chief personality chapters that would mark the forthcoming book—on Mr. Gandhi, the Shah of Iran, the Emperor of Japan, and so on. This helped mightily to ameliorate the financial problem. At the same time it meant double work. The *Digest* made its own condensations from my chapters as I wrote them, but, in order to give time for publication in magazine form, I had to write the chief personality chapters first without regard to the body of the book into which they would fit later. Hence, in violation of all normal procedure, I found myself confronted with the problem of dealing with Mr. Nehru, let us say, long before I could tackle India as a whole. Then, when it came time to do India, I was likely to find that Mr. Nehru had to be rewritten.

From about 1933, I found out, the *Digest* had been publishing original as well as digested articles. Also, its editors had worked out a scheme whereby, acting more or less in the role of agents and eager to take advantage of expert knowledge on the part of other editors, they occasionally offered articles they were interested in to other magazines, which paid for them in the regular manner. I had an astoundingly good spread, or play, with articles marketed in this unique way. The *Atlantic* took the chapter on Manuel Quezon, and *Asia* that on Nehru; *Current History* took Chiang Kai-shek and *Harper's* printed both the Shah of Iran and the Emperor of Japan, as well as smaller articles. The *Digest* saved Mr. Gandhi just for itself. Later Chaim Weizmann, the last of my major characters, went to *Life*. Frankly, I don't know any other book in an equivalent sphere that ever had such a varied serial appearance in so many good magazines.

We did the Asia journey from west to east, starting with Palestine, but I wrote the book from east to west, starting with Japan. Clearly, Japan was the "story," because of its aggression against China, and I wanted to lead off with a "strong" personality chapter. Hirohito was a good choice. I have just said that news writing and book writing are utterly different, but, even so, in those days I always tried to make each chapter of a book a "story," that is, give it a *news* significance. The events to be described might have taken place years before, but I tried to give them relevance to the present. Also, I sought with infinite care to make the structure of my "stories" different throughout a book yet conforming to the same general pattern, so that I could achieve variety within unity. The reader must not be allowed a chance to grow stale. One thing that interests me in retrospect is that, before I set out, I scribbled down a table of contents for *Asia* which ran to thirty-five chapters; the actual book has thirty-six, and the order was unchanged. It is always a good thing to have a firm structure in mind.

I have already mentioned that I never had a staff or even a researcher. However, during the Asia trip I did, in three or four capitals, ask aquaintances on the spot to dig out brief who's who material on various local characters for me because I did not have time or facilities to do so myself. But the whole of this material did not run to more than a sheaf of pages, and most of it I never used. This was not because I did not trust it but because I felt uncomfortable about using research that I had not done myself. Similarly, I bought odd bits of information when I went to Latin America but made small use of it; since that time, with one exception, I have never used any outside research at all, though I am quite capable of yelling to my secretary, "For God's sake, look up the population of Korea!"*

The first-person pronoun seldom appears in either *Inside Europe* or *Inside Asia*. I was trying to lean over backward to do impersonal reports. I remember, when I returned to New York, telling a friend about a remarkable flight I had had over the Khyber Pass, standing in the open cockpit of a fighter plane. I am the least adventurous of human beings but this was undeniably an adventure, if small. My friend remarked that it would make a lively section in the book. I said I had no intention

* I should also mention that three skilled friends went over the MS. of *Asia* to help make it a better job—Stuart Chase, Archibald MacLeish, and Walter Mallory, the Executive Director of the Council on Foreign Relations in New York.

whatever of using it, and I did not do so. I felt that it had no place in a political book. Again, I tried to keep myself out of the personality chapters and seldom stressed the fact that I myself had interviewed many of the chief characters. This was in striking contrast to the accepted journalistic formula of the day, in which the interviewer usually started out with some such overblown sentence as "In an exclusive interview today Mr. So-and-so told me," etc. In my chapter on Chiang Kai-shek I scarcely even mention that I saw him in somewhat remarkable circumstances or that he had seen no other journalist for a prolonged interview in some years—not, in fact, since the Japanese War began. Nor in my Gandhi chapter did I so much as allude to the fact that I had seen the Mahatma twice. My attitude about all this has changed to a certain extent, and in books from *Inside U.S.A.* on I have on occasion used the nasty little word "I" and have even included some personal narration. And nowadays I regret sometimes that I never put into *Asia* some colorful odds and ends—like the circumstances in which we watched an air raid in Hankow, the procedures I had to go through before being received by Prime Minister Konoye of Japan, and the occasion in Bombay on which I was the excuse for the first talk Jawaharlal Nehru ever made on the radio.

Perhaps this last episode is worth a further word. When I arrived in India I had been asked to give a formal lecture, which would be broadcast, and Mr. Nehru was to introduce me. He had only recently been released from prison, and had never spoken on the air before. But I had no time—or inclination—to prepare a lecture; then I remembered that some months earlier I had written a long article for the *Saturday Evening Post* called "This Piece Is a Cheat," and for some reason had the manuscript with me. I decided to use this as my lecture. My consternation, as the phrase goes, may be imagined when, on the very day of the lecture, I discovered that copies of the *Saturday Evening Post* containing my article had just arrived in Bombay and were being prominently displayed. I had thought, of course, that my audience would assume that I had prepared something special for its benefit. I confessed all this to Mr. Nehru later, and still do not know whether he was amused. I recall another anecdote. Some twelve years later, in 1949, Mr. Nehru came to New York for the first time, and I invited him to tea with a group of friends. He answered questions at length, and I asked him one in the personal sphere. I reminded him that we had first met in Bombay in 1937, and went on, "Did you, Mr. Nehru, think then, even in your wildest dreams, that you would be prime minister of an independent India within twelve years?" With some asperity he answered, "No!"

During the Asia trip I met many of the eminent public figures whom I wrote about, whereas in the Europe days, as a junior reporter, only seldom had I had the luck of interviewing a head of state or prime minister in an important country. Luck? I am not so sure. To be received by a very prominent personage imposes a kind of reciprocal obligation. If only for reasons of good manners, it is sometimes difficult to write critically about a political figure who has been kind enough to give you a couple of hours of his precious time. A man may be politically evil but socially a delight, and there is a certain risk of succumbing to charm if you are adeptly entertained. But anyway in Asia I put my lists of questions not merely to friends and associates of the personality I was writing about, but, in many countries, to the personality himself. I saw Mr. Gandhi, Chiang Kai-shek, the Soong sisters, President Quezon of the Philippines, Dr. Weizmann in Jerusalem, and many others. I missed Ibn Saud, the Shah of Iran, and the Emperor of Japan. Years later I did meet the Emperor of Japan, but the circumstances were different.

II

The writing of *Inside Asia,* as I have said, went swiftly, if only because I was so passionately interested in it, and the book was published in June, 1939. It did well but not so well as *Europe.* The continent of Europe was coming closer to us daily, but Asia was still a long way off. What pleased me most was the critical reception. I thought the Asia experts would annihilate me; they did not. Pearl Buck wrote a letter about it to Canfield which I still remember with much appreciation, and so, among critics at large, did Van Wyck Brooks. One curiosity is that *Inside Asia* once led the nonfiction best-seller list in the New York *Herald Tribune* while *Inside Europe* was still on it. Presently—another pleasure—I found that *Asia* was reaching some Very Important People. Joseph Barnes told me that there were three copies of it on the plane that took Wendell Willkie around the world in 1942, and it seems that a copy of the revised edition was seen resting on Mr. Truman's desk when he made his V-J Day speech in 1945. On the whole, I think that *Asia* is probably the best of the Inside books, from a technical point of view, although I should add that I haven't looked at it carefully for many years. Even today readers mention what they call its sound natural balance and vitality.

Several oddities attended translations of *Asia,* of which nine appeared in all. More would probably have come had not the war intervened. The Dutch edition—a reflection of the times—had to be published in Indonesia. There was no French edition because by the time the French got around to thinking about it the country was ruled by Vichy, which would have nothing of me. A souvenir I treasured for many years until somebody pilfered it was the American edition as it appeared in Tokyo bookshops. The customs or censorship authorities went through *each* copy shipped to Japan and with the utmost precision and meticulousness razored out of each some two hundred passages before the books were released for sale. The cuts were mostly of lines which referred personally to the Emperor (almost the whole of the first chapter), or of material stressing Japanese military aims in China and Southeast Asia. My memory is that everything about the Kwantung army in Manchuria, even down to *half* of some sentences, was cut. What light this sheds on Japanese character! Imagine the amount of physical labor it must have cost the customs people! Would book purchasers of any other nationality buy a book that had been scissored apart? And did not the very fact that the books were physically mutilated nullify the intent of the authorities by provoking curiosity and further interest?

Inside Asia had adventures in China too. Not only was a Chinese translation published (pirated, of course), which did well, but a publishing house in Shanghai went to the extraordinary length of publishing it *in English* as well. "Publishing" is not quite the right word. What these lively pirates did was to *photograph* the American edition and reproduce it by a lithographic process on cheap paper. Except for the fact that the binding and jacket were made of poor material, the books were identical. When copies of the regular American and British editions reached the China coast, they had to be priced at $5.00 or more, whereas the identical book, as manufactured by the nimble and enterprising Chinese, was available for 20 cents. Needless to say, Harper and Hamilton sales were not copious. In its own small way this story is, I dare say, as revealing about the intricacies of Chinese business habits as the one I have just told about Japan is about things Japanese.

This reminds me of another story. One day in Shanghai an American friend living there said that she wanted to have a small dinner party for me so that I might meet my Chinese publisher, editor, agent, and translator. At that moment I had no idea that any of these persons existed. The dinner duly took place, and indeed it was an amiable occasion. I have never had a better Chinese meal, and my four Chinese collaborators proved to be men of wit, charm, and substance. Of course not one word was uttered by them in regard to rights, contract, payment of royalties, or the like, nor was I so crude or commercial-minded as to bring up any such indelicate topics. What makes this anecdote more pertinent is that precisely the same thing happened in Hong Kong twelve years later, in 1950, when, again, I was amiably confronted at a party with my Chinese publisher, translator, and so forth (different ones now), who had flown from Formosa for the occasion and who ceremoniously presented me with the Chinese translation of one of my recent books, *Behind the Curtain,* which I did not even know had been translated into Chinese, but which they had blithely pirated. And again, of course, there were no words about anything so vulgar as permission, rights, or royalties. Twelve years after this—in 1962—I had one more encounter with the Chinese, when I saw for the first time their pirated copies *in English* of *Inside Russia Today* and *Inside Europe Today.* All this refers to the Nationalist Chinese on Taiwan, of course—not to those immoral Communists on the mainland.

III

As soon as I finished proofs on *Asia* I hurled them at Harper's and set out for Europe holding commissions from the North American Newspaper Alliance, *Reader's Digest,* and NBC. The idea was that I should treat myself to a quick glimpse of Europe on the eve of war; one British journalist described the trip as my "personal encirclement of Hitler" and said that presumably I would deal with both the hammer and the "swastickle." As a matter of fact not only did I visit all eleven of the countries that lay on the periphery of Hitler's enormously swollen Reich at that time but, at mild risk, even managed to spend a few days secretly in Germany itself. By what seemed to be an almost alarming coincidence I arrived in Moscow a day or two before the Russo-German pact, and, after complicated experiences in the three Baltic States, which I had never visited before, reached London just before war was declared, on the last plane out of Sweden, in September, 1939. In Poland I had a ball-before-Waterloo dinner with Colonel Beck, the ill-fated Foreign Minister; in France I met Laval, Daladier, and Blum for the first time; in England I had a talk with Churchill, who was then First Lord of the Admiralty. But I would rather not go into anecdotal details about these various encounters, because this reminiscence is supposed to be restricted strictly to the Inside books, and is not about the rest of me at all.

IV

Inside Latin America followed. Archibald MacLeish, who was working at the time on *Fortune* and had returned recently from a mission to Chile and Argentina, urged this book upon me, and it was a project that followed logically from the other books. The person who helped me most was Sumner Welles, who was at that time Undersecretary of State. I called upon him in Washington, never having met him before; it took him about thirty seconds to grasp what I was after. He proceeded then to cover both sides of the fence for me: first, by sending out an instruction to every American head of mission on the Latin-American continent to be on the lookout for me; second, by giving me introductions to a formidable miscellany of Latin-American leaders in each country. Mr. Welles wanted me to do the trip from east to west, that is, to see Brazil, Argentina, and so on, before going to the countries on the west coast. I think he felt that I might be shocked by the primitiveness of the Andean countries if I saw them first. But I followed my own impulse, overruled him, and, after starting out in Mexico and Central America, did the west coast first. The Welles introductions gave me a red carpet everywhere. This was something quite new for me. I had started out for Asia with exactly three letters of introduction, all informal, but now I had virtually a semiofficial status.

This was the winter of 1940-41. I traveled alone, and visited all twenty of the Latin-American republics as well as Trinidad and Puerto Rico. When I returned Mr. Welles arranged to have me see President Roosevelt; he thought F.D.R. might be interested in my report. I had never met the President for a private talk, and the time allotted me was limited. At once I sought to gain his attention by mentioning that I had visited all twenty Latin-American countries; he gave me a long quizzical look and, with his cigarette traversing a slow arc, said, "What? All twenty? Even *Paraguay?*" I don't know whether I told Mr. Roosevelt so, but for the accuracy of the record I should certainly add here that some of the twenty got extremely short shrift, which I lamented. I am still too embarrassed to put into cold print exactly how many hours I spent in the two countries where I had the briefest stays, Venezuela and Honduras. This was the first book for which I kept a list, fairly complete, of all the people I met on a trip who gave me information. It runs to 417 names, which works out to roughly twenty interviews per country—not enough. One detail is that of the twenty Latin-American heads or acting heads of state I saw seventeen. Another is that I crossed the Andes four times in DC-3's that seemed as frail as canoes.

The trip took about five months and the writing went quickly (March-August, 1941), although I was much upset by personal problems and most of my other thoughts were occupied by the war in Europe. This was the first Inside that did not begin with a personality chapter. I found that I had to start out with a general explanation of the subject, if only because I had to explain it to myself. I suppose, to be honest, that I was not particularly interested in Latin America. The only Latin Americans I met who seemed to me important personages on the highest level were former president Lázaro Cárdenas of Mexico, Haya de la Torre, the Aprista leader in Peru, and above all Luis Muñoz Marín in Puerto Rico, a magnificent human (as well as political) being. All three are, a fact not without interest, men strongly of the left—men indisputably of the people. I experienced all manner of odd personal encounters. In Nicaragua the dictator of the day, Anastasio Somoza, put on a military review for me—what an idiocy! Arriving in the Argentine from Uruguay, I was physically searched by the customs authorities, the only time in my life this has occurred. The Argentines thought that I was a cocaine smuggler. Again, I wish I had space for memories of other episodes, such as the lunch in Buenos Aires given for me at the American Embassy, which was a splendid occasion except for the fact that I wasn't there. And I wish I could print a little poem by Ambassador Norman Armour about me and the foot-and-mouth disease.

I managed to do a certain amount of writing while actually en route in Latin America, but not as much as during the Asia trip. I did a broadcast from Mexico City and wrote several news stories for NANA and the *New York Times,* including a piece about Guatemala and one article which I have never been able to forget, on Paraguay, because having to write it ruined several days in Brazil. I cannot remember whether, on my return, *Reader's Digest* handled this book as it had handled *Asia,* but various chapters appeared in various magazines. The *Digest* itself used no fewer than seven articles, and others were printed by *Foreign Affairs, Current History, Look, Harper's Bazaar,* and *Harper's.*

Inside Latin America was published in October, 1941, got an unexpectedly good critical reception, and had a large distribution by the Book-of-the-Month Club. Translations, however, were few—only three in all. No French edition could, of course, be published in France itself because of the German occupation, but a French translation called *L'Amérique Latine* did appear in Montreal. I have reason to believe that a Russian edition exists, but have never seen a copy. Several Soviet diplomats whom I knew in the old days when it was possible to have frank talk with Russians told me that they had read it in Russian. The reception in Latin America itself was mixed. It was instantly banned in Panama and the Dominican Republic, where I had had the sense, even then, to see that Trujillo was a special kind of monster, and was severely criticized in several other countries, particularly Argentina. Mexico, Chile, and Brazil were friendlier, and a few years after the book was published I had a letter from a correspondent in La Paz, Bolivia, saying that a bookstore there was offering it in a choice of three languages—English, French, and Spanish.

By this time I knew that, when critics treated me harshly, they would seize on three points; this became clear after *Latin America* and has held true ever since to a degree. First, I am "superficial." But I had to cove a broad surface, in that I was dealing with whole continents; the scholar-specialist who spends fifteen years on a work on a single village in Peru is much more superficial if you think in terms of the large. My purpose was educational in a much more comprehensive sense—to inform substantial numbers of readers on basic facts and themes applicable everywhere, to provide a compass, a political guide, a compendium of information, useful on the broadest level continent by continent. Then, too, I like to recall a remark by André Gide to the effect that, unless a book bores you, you are apt to think there is no depth in it. I would be more highly regarded than I am in some academic circles if it were not for the fact that many people seem to find me readable. I might add, in passing, that I don't think anybody ever called *U.S.A.* or *Africa* "superficial." Second, I am "inaccurate." This charge I am prepared to deny. Any work containing thousands upon thousands of facts will be bound to contain a few minor slips. Maybe I called a street an avenue, or vice versa. Once in *Russia* I made a figurative reference to a 25-kopek piece, and learned later that there is no coin of that denomination. But that in general the Inside books do maintain a high level of accuracy can scarcely be doubted. Third, I do not stay in countries long enough. I dismiss Uruguay with three days, or Brazil in three weeks. Heaven knows I would like to stay everywhere longer. But my kind of book would never get done at all if I allowed myself unlimited time. My trips would take years, and long before I finished them the material gathered in the beginning would be dead. Besides, you can see an amazing lot in a country in a day or two if you really use your legs, eyes, and ears. And what you observe is supplemented by intensive reading and other research.

V

As soon as *Latin America* was finished I flew to London to report the blitz, but—I still don't know whether to call this good luck or bad—I never saw a serious raid. I left London to fly back to the United States on an interesting date, December 7, 1941. The news of the attack on Pearl Harbor caught me at Bristol as I was about to board a Dutch plane to Portugal. When I reached New York, on the last American merchantman to leave Europe for some little time, Canfield suggested that I embark on a revision of *Inside Asia* to bring it up to date, focusing it on the war in the Pacific. This I agreed to do, and it turned out to be a long, difficult, and tedious job; I added—and subtracted—a good many thousand words. As always, Harper and Hamilton performed miracles to publish the book quickly, and it came out in 1942. But the revision did not do particularly well and we gave up any thought of attempting to keep the book alive in the manner of *Inside Europe*. Events came so fast in Asia and the Pacific that further updating was impossible.

CHAPTER III

Insidoosa

Glancing at what I have written so far I think I have given a somewhat false impression. I sound intolerably active, tidy, and efficient. The opposite is true. I am not efficient at all, and anybody close to me knows how physically lazy and self-indulgent I am. I waste a preposterous amount of time sitting inert like a blob of protoplasm. I don't think that even my worst enemy would call me a grind. My industriousness comes in spurts. While working I always managed in those days to have weekends off, cultivate friendships, and enjoy an abundant social life. There were spaces in every day. I read voluminously for fun, and even had time for bouts of illness. I have seldom lived to full capacity. Thinking it over, I suppose that the chief difference between the activity of a person in his thirties and in his sixties is that during the thirties there always seemed to be ever so many more hours in the day.

Emil Ludwig, the German biographer, once told me when I was in my late thirties that the years between forty and sixty go like a flash. I was not quite prepared to accept this warning when he uttered it but I know now that what he said is true.

There is, to my mind, a sharp line of demarcation between the first three Insides and those that followed. I do not mean merely that the next were longer, solider and deeper-dug. My point of view was changing. Books were no longer a crazy lark. I prepared my way more elaborately and did much more systematic research. My approach became less newsy, and my scale broader. I was becoming less interested in personalities, although personality certainly plays a role in all my books, and more interested in history. I cared less about what a dictator ate for breakfast. What I sought, no matter with what inadequacy, was to give a more complete picture of a city or a state or a nation than I had ever attempted before. I wanted, in all diffidence, to make countries, not merely people, come to life. Recently a Belgian official said that I was a "master" of what he called the *national* profile; this is not true, because I am not a master of anything, not even of my own mind, but it is true that I was beginning to feel my way toward a new objective—to bring states and countries, as well as statesmen and politicians, back alive.

After the revision of *Inside Asia* I spent a year broadcasting, and then flew to Europe in the summer of 1943 as a war correspondent for NANA and the Blue Network. I decided to go to the Mediterranean theater, not the Pacific, and never saw the Pacific war at all. I was lucky, and arrived in Malta and Sicily just in time to cover the first Allied invasion of occupied Europe (Sicily), but I was not much interested in spot news and my experience was not substantial. Still, I had startlingly good opportunities for observing Eisenhower, Mountbatten, Montgomery, and some other military behemoths at close range; I wrote articles for *Collier's* and *Reader's Digest* (on Ascension Island, a secret stop on the U.S. air route to Africa), and gathered material for two small books. Nothing is ever real to me unless it is in book form. Back in America I resumed work on the radio, but my heart and backsides were not in it. I knew by this time that it was now or never. The United States, like a cobra, lay before me, seductive, terrifying, and immense. For years I had been planning an *Inside U.S.A.* and I knew that if I deferred it any longer the opportunity might be lost forever. The idea had been teasing me, tormenting me, for years; but every time I approached it I drew back.

In fact, *Inside U.S.A.* was the hardest task I ever undertook. I quit my job on the radio and got to work. It is still bewildering to me that no writer before me had ever thought of doing this book. A state-by-state survey of the United States was surely a feasible project. Nor has anybody, with the exception of one French journalist, ever tried since to do what I did in 1944-1947. My book is still the only state-by-state account of the United States that exists in English. Nobody could be more aware than I of its manifest shortcomings. For instance, it contains the most serious misjudgment of a personality I have ever made—a downgrading of Earl Warren. I never met him, was misled about him by various sources in California, and did not grasp his true, splendid stature. A more general glaring flaw in the work is malproportion. It is not an altogether well-ordered book, as *Asia* was. This is partly because it is only a fragment, long as it is, of what came to be planned as a two-volume venture. Several personalities got too much space, and some who properly belonged in it never got into it at all because I was saving them for what I hoped would be a second volume, *Inside Washington.*

Let me go into this in more detail. Originally, I envisaged a single book in two parts. The first part would cover the structure of government in Washington and survey the American political scene from the national level. I planned to start with the President—two chapters about Mr. Roosevelt. Then I hoped to proceed through the Cabinet and executive departments of government, the Congress, the Supreme Court, pressure groups, agriculture, labor, industry, and so forth. The result would have been a kind of civics text hinged on news and personalities. The second section of the book would comprise the 48-state survey. After a few weeks in Washington I decided to do the trip covering the states first. I do not know why. For some reason I like to do things backwards. I read magazines—even some books—back to front. Before long as I traveled I perceived that I was accumulating such a huge burden of material, state by state, that the book would have to be two books. One volume could not hold it all. Then, because much of my research was highly perishable, I decided that Part Two of the book (the states, as originally conceived) should be written and published first. And this is what became *Inside U.S.A.* Alas, I have never proceeded to doing the second book, *Inside Washington,* which should have been the first.

But my original concept did produce a splinter, if you can call a book of 180,000 words a splinter. This was *Roosevelt in Retrospect,* which is still my favorite among all my books. Soon after *Inside U.S.A.* was published it occurred to me that I had gathered a great deal of material on Mr. Roosevelt which should not be permitted to go to waste. I thought first in terms of a brief profile, but the project expanded; I never dreamed when I started it that it would grow into a full-sized book and take me more than a year of hard work to write. Then, too, I might mention another splinter, a minor splinter called *The Story of TVA.* While visiting the Tennessee Valley Authority I conceived a passionate admiration for this undertaking. It is one of the comparatively few institutions that have ever really stirred me. My chapter about it in *Inside U.S.A.* reflected this emotion, and the TVA authorities asked for permission to publish it as a pamphlet. It is distributed locally as a guide, originally priced at 25 cents, and has been available to visitors to the region ever since.

II

Now back to the parent book, *Inside U.S.A.* itself. Altogether, work on it took me from the summer of 1944 until the spring of 1947. First came a period of systematic preparation, and I then spent thirteen months visiting the forty-eight states. I did the trip in three installments —first, a kind of dry run covering New England; second, a long swing through the South, the Pacific coast, the mountain states, and the Middle West; third, the Atlantic seaboard. I began writing in January, 1946, and finished fifteen months later, in March, 1947. Harper's had been setting the last part of the work chapter by chapter, and publication in America followed quickly on May 28, 1947. Most of the writing had to be done under the pressure of acutely difficult and painful circumstances: my son Johnny's long illness which I have described in *Death Be Not Proud.*

I knew from the start that *Inside U.S.A.* would be a difficult task and I went through several procedures that I had never tried before and have not attempted since. First, I prepared a fairly elaborate syllabus of what I hoped to write. This was mimeographed, and I sent it out to a number of people all over the country, perhaps a hundred, asking for their comments, if any. This provoked a remarkably lively response. Several friends went to the trouble of sending me long, well-considered memoranda, from which I derived chastening profit. A list of some of their names appears in "Acknowledgments" at the end of *Inside U.S.A.* Then I called on twenty or thirty senators, congressmen, and other public officials in Washington to sound them out about their states and ask them to put me on to people whom I should try to meet. Soon I had the names of a hundred or more men and women to look up. Similarly in New York I went to citizens in such fields as industry, labor, communications, race relations, and the like, asking for introductions throughout the country. The late Walter White of the National Association for the Advancement of Colored People helped me substantially with stimulating and corrective conversation; so did Professor Raymond Walsh of the CIO; so did people as variously placed as Thomas W. Lamont, Hamilton Fish Armstrong, Louis Fischer, H. L. Mencken, Thomas K. Finletter, colleagues like Dorothy Thompson, and, as on previous adventures, Archibald MacLeish.

Next—I still shudder slightly to think of this—I wrote to all forty-eight governors explaining my mission and asking three questions which I thought were artful: (1) How does your state differ from all the rest? (2) What does your state contribute to the Union as a whole? (3) What led you into public life and what do you consider to be your chief accomplishment? Out of forty-eight governors, forty-seven replied.

Later, I sent out various chapters of the manuscript for criticism, correction, and amendment to people—about forty—whom I had met in various watchtowers throughout the country and who had given me material. Some of these names are also given in the passages that conclude *Inside U.S.A.* Several friends returned these chapters magnificently slashed to bits, which meant that I had to rewrite them. One person who helped staunchly was the late Senator Richard L. Neuberger of Oregon. In fact, Dick Neuberger was the only person but me who ever actually wrote part of an Inside book. He became agitated by my passages on the Pacific Northwest and noticed some things that I had missed; promptly he sat down and typed off three or four paragraphs which I proceeded to insert into my text. (I have made a little slip in the above; I have just remembered that Jennifer Chatfield, then of the Brooklyn Museum of Fine Arts, did a brief draft for me of the section on African art and music in *Inside Africa,* part of which I used.) Another substantial aid during the actual writing of the book was a series of small stag dinners which Canfield gave at the Harvard Club. The guests were Frederick Lewis Allen, then the editor of *Harper's Magazine,* John Fischer, and Thomas K. Finletter, now Ambassador to NATO. These expert gentlemen briefed me on sections of the country they knew best, checked my lists of generalizations, helped sketch out treatment of projected chapters and put me back on the track when I had wandered off.

But now I am getting ahead of my story. What I should be describing is my trip or trips. I did visit all the states, but I must admit that several of them got very short handling, particularly Idaho, Maryland, and Arkansas. But of cities in the country which had a population of more than 200,000 at that time I saw all but five. Also, as goes without saying, I visited a great many smaller communities and made several journeys off the urban track, for instance to the ranch lands of Texas, the power system in the Columbia River Valley, and agricultural areas in the Middle West. One of the virtues

I brought to the job, besides curiosity, was ignorance. Until the trip I had never in my life been in Denver, New Orleans, Atlanta, Memphis, or Salt Lake City, and except to pass through on a train or fly over, I had never been in Oklahoma, Montana, Kentucky, Delaware, or the Dakotas. As I wrote subsequently in my introduction, all of this did, at least, give me the advantage of a fresh eye. Not only was I trying to write for the man from Mars; I was one.

Never before had I taken a project so seriously, although I know now that I did not take it seriously enough; my activity was always subject to indulgences and interrupted by bouts of confusion or apathy. One thing making for difficulty was the national traffic jam caused by the war. I wrote months in advance to hotels in every city I intended to visit (in those days hotels would not accept guests for longer than five days) and inflicted on my secretary at that time, Nancy Barnett—who, incidentally, typed the whole of *Inside U.S.A.* twice and parts of it three and four times—a ghastly lot of nuisance over similar matters. I wrote to every airline in the United States, to stave off the danger of being bumped on flights, and dealt with other problems in logistics. Gasoline rationing was still in force, and travel by automobile was difficult, although on several laps the local authorities shoved me from one state to the next in police cars. Moreover, I had to cling closely to a prearranged itinerary, and I went through anguish wondering in advance if my allotment of time for Minnesota, say, was not too little, or for South Dakota not too much.

I did little writing while I was actually en route except, of all things, a long article far off my track on the sharp deterioration then beginning (early 1945) in relations between the United States and Russia. This had nothing whatever to do with my book, but my disappointment and apprehension about rising tensions in American-Soviet affairs were so acute that I had to express myself somehow. My line was that, if Washington and Moscow did not succeed in making a real peace, Hitler—even in death—would turn out to have won the war. Writing this article ruined a week in New Orleans, but I felt better when I had delivered myself of it.

It was interesting, as the U.S.A. trip continued, to see how my reception differed from that which I had had in Europe, Asia, and Latin America. I found that Americans were more accessible than Europeans, more sophisticated in regard to some of the inquiries of journalism, and prouder of their communities. Most Americans are house-proud. A good deal of political naïveté was, however, discernible even among those sophisticated. Time and again I found that citizens resented it when I asked, "Who runs this community?", did not understand the question, or answered it determinedly with some such pious cliché as "the people." They did not catch it that the purpose of my question was to break concepts like "the people" down.

Of course, different sections of the country had their own different patterns. It is certainly a minor criterion, but I was fascinated by the fact that, if my recollection is correct, I was never once interviewed by any local newspaper in New England, New York, Pennsylvania, or Southern California. But I was widely sought after and written about all over the Middle West, the mountain states, the South (where I was front-page news in almost every city) and, in particular, Texas. I was even invited to address a joint session of the Texas legislature!

I had no idea how well known I was, unbecoming as it is for me to say this myself, until this journey. Several times people said pleasant things. One was Dr. Douglas

Southall Freeman, the biographer of Lee. When, after a talk with him in Richmond, I thanked him, he replied, "But think of all that you have given *us*!" In Philadelphia I called on Judge Finletter (Tom's father), who said that my chief quality was that I had the knack of convincing the reader that what I wrote was the truth. In Memphis, Tennessee, I met a veteran Scripps-Howard editor, Edward J. Meeman. We talked most of one afternoon and I sketched some of my further plans. His last remark was "If only you can do for this country what you have done for Asia!" Then he added that I was doing *U.S.A.* at exactly the right moment, "because what is going on inside us will soon dominate the world." This was a prescient remark.

I might also add that one senator (McKellar) threw me out of his office ("Sir, I will now show you the door!") and one governor, after my book came out, wrote me the rudest letter I have ever received.

For a long time I was perplexed by the problem of describing myself. If I simply sent a wire asking for an appointment with somebody in the next town without explaining who I was, I felt that I was being intolerably vain in assuming that people would know my name, but, on the other hand, if I stated my identity in a telegram, this might seem intolerably pretentious. I had to draw a line between two modesties, mock and real. From Denver I telegraphed Alf M. Landon in Topeka, my next stop, with the words, "Am author Inside Europe etc. can I see you Topeka Friday." Mr. Landon's reply was swift and to the point. "We are not hicks in Kansas and know perfectly well who you are. Come to dinner six o'clock."

This was a brilliant occasion. Six or seven guests were present, all hard-shell Republicans. Argument was furious, and I had a productive time. The next morning

Mr. Landon telephoned me to say that he felt that I had heard only one side of the Kansas story, and should know more. So he asked me to come to dinner again *that* night, and this time he assembled a different group —all Democrats and liberals! Mostly these were professors from the University of Kansas. I have always thought that this was a nicely typical American episode. Maybe it could happen in England, but I doubt if any public figure in any other country would go through such a procedure merely to see that a visiting writer was briefed on both sides of a local situation.

Then I will not forget an encounter I had with E. H. Crump in Memphis, the last of the great city bosses. I did not want to see him, because it was my gentle intention to make him a villain and I did not wish to be under any obligation to him. My astonishment and embarrassment were considerable when, after a couple of days in Memphis, I was called on the telephone by none other than Boss Crump himself, personally, who paid me extravagant compliments and then went on to say that he seriously thought I could not possibly get a fair picture of Tennessee without the advantage of conversation with him. So I went over to call on the old man, with his streaming pyramid of cotton-white hair and cheeks and chin like three hard red apples, and had an illuminating hour.

Early one day the telephone rang in my hotel room in Minneapolis. Apparently the morning newspaper had printed a small item announcing that I was in town. I had not done my homework carefully, and did not identify the name of the caller. His voice boomed cheerfully into the telephone, with the words that he would drop in to see me at five that afternoon. I did my best to avoid this commitment, on the assumption that an interview with this unknown would be a waste of time. I said that

I had another engagement. I tried to wriggle out. My efforts were vain. My caller's voice became more buoyantly insistent. Finally I said that I would call him back, and asked for his name and number. The voice replied with surprise, "Why, I'm Hubert Humphrey—I'm the mayor!" Mr. Humphrey arrived at five accompanied by several expert assistants, and they talked about Minneapolis and its problems for three and a quarter hours. I have never had a more acute and provocative briefing. Soon after this Mr. Humphrey advanced into the national scene, and, as everybody knows, is today one of the ablest, most liberal, and most courageous senators Minnesota has ever sent to Washington.

One thing that struck me was that, even though the United States has been written about very copiously indeed by a couple of thousand writers over the past hundred and fifty years, there are still such substantial gaps in our national knowledge. I wonder if there has ever been a good biography of Hiram Johnson. How I would have liked to find a vivid and readable serious study of American railroads, or the early muckraking phase in American journalism, or the Mormon church. (Incidentally, of all the cities that were affronted by *Inside U.S.A.* when it came out, Salt Lake City was affronted most.) I was struck too by how little even well-informed people knew about their local politics. I went, for instance, through the length and breadth of California and never once heard the name of Arthur Samish, although at that time Mr. Samish was the undisputed political boss of the state. But perhaps the fault was mine in this case, and I was being a bad reporter in that I failed to ask about him.

If I should start noting down some of the picturesque episodes attending the U.S.A. journey, this memorandum would be endless. At a small dinner in Cincinnati I began by asking my stock question: "Who runs this place?" As always, I was trying to find out what makes *power* in a community. Sometimes questions like "Who runs Cincinnati?" or "What *really* goes on here?" will produce lively discussion, but this time an embarrassed silence followed. Then I discovered that everybody who *did* run Cincinnati was right there in that room, but hated to admit that they ran it. When we broke up at midnight one guest said, "I don't know about you, but I have learned more about Cincinnati tonight than I've learned in twenty years."

Everywhere I went friends sent me on to other friends. Acquaintances became, so to speak, participants in my project. A banker in Des Moines would tell me about a banker in Spokane. I had some rewarding experiences —from a talk with old Josephus Daniels in Raleigh, North Carolina, on the day Roosevelt died, to a trip to Sauk Centre, Minnesota, the original Main Street, promoted by none other than Sinclair Lewis himself. I discovered how rich America was in splendid human beings, from a Roman Catholic archbishop in San Antonio to a radical editor in Madison, Wisconsin. I was lucky enough to enter into friendships with men like David E. Lilienthal, who at that time was head of TVA, and Paul G. Hoffman, the president of Studebaker. Then, too, I still feel keen regret, even resentment, at having missed some people. Several of these were not eminent, at least not eminent on a political level. They were simply men and women who had aroused my curiosity or admiration, and whom I felt it would be a pleasure to meet—a folklore specialist in Dallas, a railroad man in Omaha, an editor in Atlanta, a rabbi in Cleveland, a farm leader in Montana. Also, I still feel bitter regret at having had to leave things out of *Inside U.S.A.* There should have been more in it about shipping on the Great Lakes, forest fires, trails, corruption in labor unions, Kentucky politics, inland waterways, and national parks; also lacking is an analysis of some industrial agglutination, although I was perhaps saving this for what I hoped would be the second volume.

Something else I bitterly regret to this day is that, just as I was fairly getting under way on the U.S. trip, an invitation was suddenly proffered in the last days of the war to fly to Europe as a guest of the Air Force, and thus see at first hand the final act of the Götterdämmerung I had watched build up for more than twenty years. The trip was organized by the Association of Radio News Analysts in New York, and we were to have our own special plane. No junket could have been more abundantly exciting, and it would have cost me no more than a couple of months. Canfield urged me to go, but I felt that I could not in good conscience interrupt my work on *U.S.A.* I have hated myself for this priggish decision ever since.

When I look back to the U.S.A. journey now, my dominant thought is that I wish I could do it over. I would like extremely to visit Wilson Wyatt in Louisville again, have lunch with Roy Roberts and his staff on the Kansas City *Star,* see the wheat fields in eastern Washington, which are the exact color of an *omelette aux fines herbes,* partake of palatial hospitality in Denver, and explore the back streets of Atlanta in a squad car with Governor Ellis Arnall. The state I enjoyed most was, I think, Montana. How I would have liked to stay longer there! The state where people were most suspicious of me was Iowa, with Mississippi a close second. The most agreeable, distinguished dinner party I attended took place in Boston, with one in Charleston, South Carolina, as runner-up. The most beautiful house I saw was in Princeton, New Jersey, and the best restaurants I found were in Milwaukee and

San Francisco. Local phenomena that really staggered me were pheasants in South Dakota and mellifluous effrontery of politicians in Pennsylvania and Massachusetts. The best interviewer I encountered was a young woman in Cheyenne, Wyoming; the worst, a brash youngster in the Texas ranch country. Almost everything else in Texas was a delight—including a weird adventure in Amarillo and a remark by one of my hosts in Fort Worth (or was it Houston?) to the effect that *Inside U.S.A.* should be two books, one just about Texas, the other for all the other forty-seven states.

III

At last my road work was done, and in January, 1946, I started writing. Periods of dogged endeavor, joy, and despair alternated. I worked best at night and on Sundays, when interruptions were fewer. Night after night I plodded back to the office I had in those days on East 49th Street, after a hurried dinner, and started work anew. Sometimes it seemed that I was the only person still there, with a light still burning, in our entire building as eleven P.M. became midnight, and then one o'clock, two o'clock, three o'clock in the morning. I ached with frustration and self-pity. But weariness was compensated for by exhilaration. I was capable in those days of feats of endurance far beyond me now. I researched, wrote, revised, and checked one chapter of *Inside U.S.A.* in a single day. There were times when nothing could stop me. I would finish writing Wyoming with a whoop and without taking five minutes off start Colorado.

Once, near the end, I took a young pretty girl to the theater. She was astonished when, a few minutes before the curtain was to rise, I stumbled out of my seat and muttered apologetically that I *had* to go back to work.

I could not bear not to finish that night the segment of the book ("Sources" in the Bibliography) I was engaged upon, and which was almost done. It was the dreariest kind of drudgery, but it fascinated me. Anyway, there was no room in my mind for anything else. I promised my friend to return before the final curtain, if possible, and begged her to excuse me, et cetera, et cetera. If my memory is right, I arrived back at the theater just as the performance finished. I was not contrite at all, but happy. "Sources" was finished too. The show was *The Iceman Cometh.* The girl still speaks to me.

When I finished *Inside U.S.A.* I hoped to proceed at once with *Inside Washington.* I happened to be in Chicago a week before the book was published, and automatically, like a person driven, I filled up spare time by calling on several local dignitaries, in order to be starting research for the new volume without delay, although I had scarcely had a day off for three years. I was coasting on momentum. Then I went forthwith to Washington to see some people I had missed, like John L. Lewis and J. Edgar Hoover. But I never used the interviews they gave me, because the Washington book has never been written. I was overcome by Mr. Lewis' majesty, and was fascinated to observe that Mr. Hoover had a wooden bust of Dante in his office, used a small silver vise as a paperweight, and pronounced the word "dossier" dosseer.

I could not have done *Inside U.S.A.* without, first of all, the utmost in co-operation from Canfield of Harper's; second, without support from *Reader's Digest.* This was arranged by Carl Brandt—with whom, unhappily, I later parted company. The *Digest* paid my expenses for part of the trip, and, going beyond this, also gave me a stipend for a year. I am not sure that Pleasantville got as substantial a return from this investment as it should have had, because, for some reason or other, it did not print much from *U.S.A.*—only three articles in all (on Texas, Mr. Truman when he became President, and Boss Crump). Nor did I have as much success in placing chapters in other magazines as I had had with previous books. But *Harper's Magazine,* my oldest ally, printed articles on Texas and Harold Stassen, and other magazines gave hospitality to Saltonstall, Vandenberg, and Dewey. My favorite chapter was the one on LaGuardia. It still chafes me that I was never able to sell it anywhere.

Canfield's faith kept me alive in more ways than one. The fiber of this heroic personage may be judged from the fact that, when the book was already more than 480,000 words long, two-thirds the length of the Bible, and at a moment when we were desperately striving to meet a crucial deadline, he calmly returned the chapter I had just sent in on Maryland with a little note to the effect that it seemed a bit short and could I add a few words more.

My order of writing was New England first, then Texas, then California, then a few of the personality chapters because I thought these would be the easiest to sell to magazines. Next I started on the Pacific Northwest and came backwards through the West until I reached Kansas and Missouri. From that time on it was a question of pushing slowly ahead—the Middle West, Southwest, and the Atlantic seaboard—and filling gaps in the South. I did not decide to begin the actual book with California (the obvious choice would have been New York) until halfway through the trip, on a hot lonely day in Butte, Montana.

Naturally Harper's and I both hoped strenuously that *Inside U.S.A.* would be taken by the Book-of-the-Month Club, which it was. But a tale hangs on this. The Book-of-the-Month Club works well in advance.

We had to aim at a certain month. The book was so timely that we could not afford to submit it and then delay publication for many months, if it was accepted. So we set a grim, irrevocable deadline for November, 1946, put into type all the chapters that had then been written, something more than half of the whole, bound them in paper, and submitted them. On the basis of this the Book-of-the-Month accepted the book as its selection for June, 1947. This produced fantastic complications. I have faced many deadlines, but never any so formidably ironclad as this one now impending. Clearly, if I did not finish the rest of the book in time, there would be no Book-of-the-Month for the scheduled month, an advent as scandalous as if a month should appear without a moon. We set March 15, 1947, as the final deadline. Then everything I wrote went into type as soon as I wrote it. On the same day, I might well (a) be writing New Jersey; (b) doing research for the next state, Delaware; (c) checking New York, which I had just finished; and (d) reading *proofs* on Ohio. Also, everything had to be submitted to our libel lawyer, and some of the text (e.g., on California) that I had written the year before had to be laboriously worked over. I will never forget my dismay at having to unpack, dredge out, and scrutinize again my California notes, which I thought I had finished with forever.

Other bizarre complications had been occurring. I have made the point that the Book-of-the-Month got a large section of the book in advance. We wanted to make this a fair sampling of the text as a whole and felt it imperative to include at least one chapter on the South, which, at the time, I had not yet begun to write. So, at the extreme last moment of the last hour of that phase of the work, in November, 1946, I wrote Chapter 40, about the South in general, and, in order to cover some specific states as well, I followed this with Chapter 42, which describes Virginia, Georgia, and the Carolinas. Then, several months later, I had the job of doing Chapter 41, which was about the Negro problem and had to be sandwiched between Nos. 40 and 42, which also dealt copiously with the Negro and were already written and in type, without duplicating anything in them. This proved to be an almost comically arduous task. Finally, more trouble. Our second and utterly final deadline was, as I say, March 15, 1947. But in the intervening months much had happened all over the country, particularly (it maddeningly seemed) in the states that were already closed, like Georgia, and somehow I had to deal with all this new material and squeeze it in. We were forced to update state after state in proof.

From first to last we had five copies of my first draft of each chapter typed—or, at the end, when the MS had to go straight to the printer without delay, like a story in a newspaper—five sets of galley proofs. One copy went to Canfield. I have never had an editor in the usual sense at Harper's; Canfield is my editor, and indeed it is a pride of the house that he, its head, should also be an active editor. A second went to a historian whom Harper's employed to check me for accuracy; a third to our libel lawyer, Alexander Lindey, with whom Cass and I spent uncounted hours; a fourth to my own watchtower friends; the fifth was mine. Then came the job of putting all this together, making the necessary changes, which were often voluminous, and writing a second draft—sometimes a third as well. The pressure became intolerable. Another chore was the chart that appears in the original *Inside U.S.A.* I still think that this shows a certain originality, although it is devastatingly nonscientific. We dropped it from the Revised Edition because it was impossible to keep it up to date. As a further example of the drudgery

I was willing to go through, I might mention that I myself, with my own eyes and fingers, for purposes of just one item on the chart, *counted* the number of people in Who's Who classified by states. Finally I dictated some nine hundred thank-you letters to people who had helped me on the trip.

One last point in the realm of the ludicrous has to do with the litany in the last chapter which mentions things I had *not* had space for in the book. But I wrote this terminal chapter long before the book itself was completed; what I was doing was to give a list of items not included in sections not yet written! As a result came several stunning little slips. After the book was published I found that I had mentioned my regret at having had to leave out half a dozen people who, as a matter of fact, were safely in. But I utterly forgot that I *had* indeed alluded to them when it came time to revise the final chapter. *The New Yorker* caught me out on this, and made mild fun.

IV

Despite everything, *Inside U.S.A.* came out in May, 1947, and at once it was clear that we had a smash hit. I could pay my debts, which were considerable. Harper's advance sale was, I was told, the largest in its history for a trade book, and one piquant detail is that Macy's in New York did 90 per cent of its book business with this single title on one day shortly after publication. All told, the book turned out to be one of the biggest nonfiction best sellers in the history of American publishing. Two important national magazines treated me to extremely unpleasant reviews, but the critical reception as a whole was probably the best I ever had. Good reviews swamped us. I had much the same feeling of bewilderment and delight reading Orville Prescott in the *New York Times* on the day of publication as I had had reading Harold Nicolson on *Europe* eleven years before. Authors can wait all their lives for a review like this of Prescott's. And Lewis Gannett gave it *two* superb reviews on consecutive days in the *Herald Tribune*. In England, too, the reception was flattering for the most part. *Time and Tide* wrote: "Mr. Gunther would be the first to agree that he is not a Tocqueville, but think what the historian has lost because Tocqueville was not a Gunther." Luckily, before I went out to buy a larger hat, I was severely beaten up by the *Listener* and the *New Statesman*.

Late that summer I spent a weekend with Sinclair Lewis at Thorvale Farm, in Massachusetts, and we lunched on Sunday with fashionable people who lived nearby. His *Kingsblood Royal* was No. 1 on the fiction best-seller list that day; my *Inside U.S.A.* was No. 1 in nonfiction. Lewis and I chuckled, wondering if any two authors had ever been at a lunch together while holding these positions. But neither of us said a word about this to our host or hostess, nor as I recall were our books mentioned by anybody in any way. Lewis himself was not always generous toward fellow authors. Years before in London, when I had been struggling with *Inside Europe* and could well have used a friendly word of encouragement, he had snarled—yes, snarled—that it would not sell 3,000 copies. Then when I started out on *U.S.A.* he predicted harshly that the task was impossible if only because it would take a man a "year" just to find out the difference between Minneapolis and St. Paul. But he liked *Inside U.S.A.* extravagantly when it appeared and gave us a magnificent one-line blurb which is still used on the jacket.

Reviews, news stories ("Gunther is all wet"), editorials,

and letters poured in all year. In many communities local pride was much abraded. For instance, I called the state capitol of New Hampshire "the ugliest I have ever seen," and an editorial writer on a Concord newspaper promptly complained, "Mr. Gunther, no one asked you to look at our State House in the first place, and if you were a gentleman, you would have kept your unkind thoughts to yourself." The cities angriest with me, aside from Salt Lake City, where the book was boycotted in several shops, were Tulsa, Houston, and, in particular, Indianapolis, because I called it the dirtiest in the United States. Warfare was conducted against me by Indianapolis for some years. For a decade scarcely a month passed without some such headline in an Indianapolis newspaper as "Gunther vs. Indianapolis," or "Debunk Gunther." People demanded that I return under the protection of an armed guard and eat my words. One healthy result was that Indianapolis, stirred by shame, started to clean itself up. So did Butte, Montana, which I had attacked for similar reasons. One thing that impressed me was the fairness of mind of most communities. I called Knoxville, Tennessee, the ugliest city in the country, and the leading newspaper there did nothing more than print a full page of photographs showing selected sites throughout the town, asking readers to decide for themselves whether or not my comment was justified. After fifteen years repercussions still come from Indianapolis and Knoxville. I had a letter as recently as March, 1962, from a Knoxville citizen still ablaze with indignation. One community, Port Angeles, Washington, threatened to sue me for libel because I wrote that it had 141 inches of rainfall a year. The correct figure is 14.1. This was a printer's error.

For years brickbats of one kind or other continued to be hurled at me, but there were rewards as well.

One city that liked me was Phoenix, Arizona, because I called it the cleanest in the United States, and Phoenix newspapers were still printing stories with headlines like "Phoenix Makes Strong Bid to Keep Cleanest City Title" several years after the book appeared. One editor in the West, succumbing to an insensate fit of enthusiasm, went so far as to suggest that the membership of the U.S. Senate should be raised from 96 to 97 so that I might be chosen as a special "extra" senator representing *all* the states. Above all, the book continued to arouse sharp *local* responses in news stories. Here are some headlines:

GUNTHER'S "INSIDE U.S.A." MAY CAUSE SOME DERISIVE CHUCKLES INSIDE BUFFALO

AUTHOR GUNTHER APPALLED AT DRINKING AND SEXUAL HABITS IN SOUTH

EXECUTIVE DENIES "INSIDE U.S.A." CHARGES ON GEORGIA MILLS

BOSTON MOST CHARMING CITY IN AMERICA, SAYS GUNTHER

WHO RUNS KANSAS? LANDON REPEATS ANSWER TO GUNTHER

BOOK FINDS MONTANA EXUBERANT, MATURING

As to letters I received, they were of such number and variety that Canfield, at one time, thought of making a pamphlet out of them. He did use several in advertisements. One angry letter from a reader in New York said that, immediately on finishing the book, he had destroyed it "through the facilities of the New York sanitation system." (This must have been quite a job if he stuffed all of it down the toilet.) And a man from Florida wrote:

> Upon the assumption that *Inside U.S.A.* was a political, economic, and sociological survey of the United States, I purchased a copy of your book. I am amazed. You insult every woman in the South and place yourself beyond the pale of common decency. I will not have this trash in my home. If you have a shred of common decency you will refund my money.

We did.

Several letters added personal touches to the record. This came from a man in Croton-on-Hudson, New York:

> I have just finished reading your . . . book, but in writing about Austin, Texas, you say that the state capitol was paid for by giving away three million acres of land in the Panhandle in lieu of money. Correct; but you do not say that the land was given to my grandfather.

Dozens of readers corrected points of style, as to wit:

> I wish to congratulate you on your *Inside U.S.A.*, but on Page 509 the comma after *Who's Who* is not needed and should be deleted.

All this taught me a lot. About a year after publication I wrote a guest column for Leonard Lyons in the New York *Post* listing some items that letters and reviews had brought to my attention, under the title "Things I Have Learned About the U.S.A. Since Writing *Inside U.S.A.*"—for instance that:

> Montana is sometimes called the "Stub-Toe State," New Mexico the "Adobe State," Delaware the "Blue Hen State," New Jersey the "Jersey Blue State," Tennessee the "Big Bend State," North Dakota the "Flickertail State," and Arizona the "Sunset State."
>
> Lancaster, Pennsylvania, was the capital of the

United States for exactly one day, and was once the chief wheat center in the country.

The city with the "shortest thermometer" is not San Diego, California, but Eureka, in Humboldt County, California.

During the second administration of President Wilson there were seven native-born Kentuckians in the U.S. Senate.

Baton Rouge, Louisiana, Olympia, Washington, Frankfort, Kentucky, and Carson City, Nevada, are (in addition to Santa Fe, New Mexico) state capitals not on a main railroad line.

The statutes of Illinois (like those of Maine) once included a provision that every public school teacher must devote half an hour a week to teach kindness to birds and animals.

Hamilton did well with the British edition of the book which, because the paper shortage in England and other postwar factors presented almost insuperable difficulties in production, was printed here and sent over to England in sheets. Presently translations into the standard languages began to come out. My French publisher was now Gallimard of the *Nouvelle Revue Française,* than which nothing can be more distinguished, and a French edition came out presently. No German translation of *U.S.A.* has ever appeared. This was a sharp disappointment. Three different contracts for an edition in German were signed with Austrian, Swiss, and German publishers, but in each case, after exhaustive preparations, the project fell through. Generally it was felt that the book was "too long" to translate. I was delighted to have a translation into Flemish, a new language for me, but I have never seen a copy of the actual book. The Chinese pirates let me alone on this one, so far as I know; the Japanese, as usual, produced promptly a handsome double volume.

In Western Europe the book came to be known as "Insidoosa" by readers who, not knowing English well, gave this quaint pronunciation to the English title. In Eastern Europe the Iron Curtain was descending at just this time. Even so, editions were prepared in both Czechoslovakia and Hungary, which I possess; I visited Prague and Budapest in 1948 and met my publishers and editors. I believe that the Hungarian edition was suppressed immediately after publication; at any rate, friends reported to me that it was unobtainable in the local bookstores. But, oddly enough, a Bulgarian edition, the first of my books to be translated into this language so far as I am aware, soon appeared in a pirated edition. *Inside U.S.A.* came out in the Russian language as well, but not in Russia. It was prepared by what was, I believe, an offshoot of the Ford Foundation in New York called the Chekhov Publishing Company. Naturally I was pleased when this organization told me that it wanted to do my book in Russian, presumably for dissemination to Russian-reading people all over the world *outside* the Soviet Union. I do not imagine that any copies could ever have been distributed in the Soviet Union itself. It added to my pleasure to hear that mine was the second book chosen for translation into Russian by the Chekhov people, the first having been Carl Sandburg's *Abraham Lincoln*. Another pleasing development was the appearance of *Inside U.S.A.* in talking records for the blind. The three previous Insides exist in bulky Braille editions, but they were never recorded. The *U.S.A.* album was issued in 1948 by the American Foundation for the Blind and, covering 97 records, was at the time the third-longest book ever issued on talking records. The first two are the Bible and *War and Peace*.

Inside U.S.A. entered still another dimension when, soon after publication, Arthur Schwartz, the composer, bought the title for a musical show, which he proceeded to write, produce, and present on Broadway, with lyrics by Howard Dietz. None other than Beatrice Lillie was the star, and it ran for almost two years in all in New York and on the road. Nothing was used directly out of my book (I was the author of exactly two words in the show, the title), and the original concept, that of a topical American revue reflecting events and attitudes in all the states, had to be modified, but I had a pungently good time for some months watching at close range the way a Broadway musical is put together. Mr. Schwartz's music was engaging, and who but Mr. Dietz would ever have thought of rhyming "Delaware" with "well aware," "Dust Bowl" with "Lust Bowl" (Reno), and "Top of the Mark" with "Yellowstone Park."

After a year or two the problem arose whether to revise *U.S.A.* (the book) or not. For a time Harper's flirted with the idea of republishing it in the form of four regional volumes—East, South, West, Middle West. For a variety of reasons this idea was given up, and I set out instead to do a straight-out revision on the model of the revisions of *Inside Europe*. This cost me ten months of the hardest kind of work, and the new edition finally appeared in 1951; it was published simultaneously by Harper's and Bantam Books (two volumes) as a paperback. The Harper edition, though in hard cover, was manufactured in the same size as the Bantam edition so that it could be printed from the same plates. The decision to make *U.S.A.* pocket size (if thick in beam) was taken after careful deliberation, and it added substantially to the continuing sale of the book because it came to be used by thousands of people as a Baedeker, and the small format made it convenient for this purpose.

Mainly, to prepare this revised edition, I relied on a large, if heterogeneous, collection of new material which I accumulated in three years on all the forty-eight states. Then, too, I used letters I still continued to receive by the hundred which pointed out errors and suggested additions or revisions; also I made use of newspaper comment and reviews. Also, of course, I tried to mend small literary slips—shifts in emphasis, pruning of superfluous language, amplifications of fact, emendations to give passages more fluidity, punch, or grace. Altogether there were no fewer than 10,000 textual changes. In tone, this revised edition (which was reissued in a different format ten years later, in 1961) is less exuberant, less sanguine, than the original, but the basic judgments remain the same.

I have sometimes been asked why I never, as promised, proceeded at once to follow *Inside U.S.A.* with its projected twin, *Inside Washington*. There are several reasons. I became immersed in other projects. I dreaded the enormous amount of physical labor involved. Aside from these and similar considerations there was another. What balked and beat me in the end was the political system of the United States. By this I mean that, since the book would take at last two years of work, I had to start writing it immediately after the formation of a new administration or it would be bound automatically to be out of date soon after publication. In order (a) to be able to write it at all I had to wait until a new administration took office and then (b) try to finish it before midterm. My only possible starting dates were January, 1953, 1957, and 1961. Unfortunately I have missed all three.

CHAPTER IV

Personal Invasion of Two More Continents

ABOUT THE INSIDES that followed I will try to be briefer. I went to Eastern Europe for *Look* and the New York *Herald Tribune* in 1948; to Japan and around the world in 1950 for *Look,* and to Western Europe late in 1951, again for *Look.* Each of these trips produced a book, but not an Inside book. I was bracing myself for another full-scale assault on another continent. Africa was my target now. I made more orderly preparations for this trip than for any I have ever undertaken, except possibly *U.S.A.* I started systematic research early in 1952, and my wife, Jane Perry Gunther, and I made the journey between September, 1952, and August, 1953. I did not finish the writing until June, 1955. I had no idea when I started *Africa* that it would turn out to be almost as long as *U.S.A.*, roughly half a million words.

The trip was fantastically onerous as well as exciting. We traveled about 40,000 miles, which is sixteen times the air distance across the United States, and made longhand notes of conversations with more than 1,500 people. We visited 105 cities or towns in 31 countries, and had 54 different trips by air. Never have I had such a crowded itinerary. In one stretch of 25 days, we slept in sixteen different beds and in one five-week period we had—breakfast excluded—exactly one meal alone. Neither the trip nor the book could have been done without my wife's help. She handled most of the logistics of the journey and spent unlimited wearisome hours in various travel bureaus. By force of character, she made me go to a couple of places, like Angola and the Hoggar country deep in the Sahara, which I would otherwise have skipped out of laziness or lack of interest. More, when we returned to the United States and I began to write in New York and Greensboro, Vermont, she provided expert and discerning editorial scrutiny of my text, page by interminable page. One thing that slowed up the writing of *Africa,* which took me longer to write than any other book has ever taken me—twenty-two months—was that I had developed cataracts in both eyes but could not dare to take time out for an operation until the work was finished.

In general, on the Africa trip (as in Russia later) we had practically every moment taken in every town. How we stood this pace I do not know. Twice we all but collapsed, if that is not too large a word, as I had once "collapsed" in Chile; my legs turned to lead. But we took no time out at all in eleven months, except for a few days in Mozambique during the middle of our visit to South Africa.

Take Nairobi as an example of our activity. Part of the first day would have to be spent on the telephone to check on appointments we hoped we had, because we never traveled with a secretary or hired one locally. On the next day, and those following, we might well have a schedule which included half a dozen appointments from about 10:30 A.M. till 6:00 and covering a range of people all the way from the whitest of white settlers to the blackest of black nationalist revolutionists. Normally we had engagements for lunch, cocktails, and dinner as well, and time for shopping and sightseeing or going to the dentist would have to be sandwiched in; also an hour with the travel man to fix up the safari we were planning later, and a few minutes, anyway, to read the local papers and send out the laundry. Further telephone calls to arrange plans, telegrams to lay out lines ahead, hotel reservations to confirm six or seven cities in advance, interviewers to see, and letters to write (there was always a ghastly backlog of correspondence) interrupted us. Then at midnight we had to take notes on what had happened during the day. The minute we boarded the plane for our next stop, split asunder between exhilaration and fatigue, out would come my briefcase, so that Jane and I could glance through our Uganda dossier before we touched ground at Entebbe. And always there were lists to make—of people seen, people to see, arrangements to verify, telegrams to send. Usually I sought to write out a series of questions to ask the political personalities we would be meeting soon. Always too there was an infernal collection of memories to write down of impressions and conversations we had had in the countries we had left behind. What a life!

II

But let me go back to the period of preparation, before the actual trip began. This occurred in New York, Washington, London, Brussels, and Paris. First we had to decide whether to do the journey clockwise or the reverse, because of considerations of climate. Climate?

Yes, not because we were timid of being hot or cold or of getting our feet wet, but because seasonal rains can fatally impede communications. Actually in Africa we went through two different winters (in Morocco and South Africa) and encountered two different rainy seasons (in Ruanda-Urundi and Liberia). Our decision was to start with Morocco and go around the continent from west to east. This it happened was the same course eventually taken by the book itself.

In Washington I sought contact with the independent African governments (there were only five at the time) which maintained missions there: Liberia, Ethiopia, Libya, Egypt, and the Union of South Africa. I called on the French and Portuguese, and had extremely helpful talks with the British, who at that time had a Colonial Attaché attached to their Washington embassy and agents who—even in that remote period—represented the Gold Coast (now Ghana) and Nigeria. African specialists in the State Department helped us considerably, and officials in the U.S. defense establishment gave us introductions to our military units in Morocco, Libya, and Eritrea. Another helper was David K. E. Bruce, then the Undersecretary of State and now Ambassador to London, who put us on to American diplomatic and consular officers throughout the whole of the African continent. In New York I sought illumination from the French and Belgians. Roger Vaurs of the French press office in New York helped to lay out our Sahara trip in one vivid afternoon, and Major C. B. Ormerod (now Sir Berkeley Ormerod), of British Information Services, paved the way for us everywhere in British Africa with his usual adroit, highly sensitive efficiency.

Next we spent three weeks in London, which, in those days, was the capital not merely of imperial but of nationalist Africa. Not only did we have long briefings in the Colonial Office, Commonwealth Relations Office, Foreign Office, Sudanese Office, and Rhodesia House but, on the other side of the street, met dozens of experts both African and non-African who represented non-official organizations, of which London is full, including some vigorous Kenya nationalists who were living in Britain—of all places!—in exile. Then David Astor, editor of the *Observer,* had us to lunch with half a dozen specialists, whose talk vastly increased our field of vision; our Tanganyika journey was, as an example, laid out in all essential details at that moment.

The British are extraordinarily adept at public relations, which of course depend on private relations. No one in London ever told us that it would happen and to this day I do not know who was responsible, but, with one exception, we were put up at Government House in every British territory we visited. This was a signal convenience from the point of view of the amenities of travel, but sometimes it produced minor embarrassments as well. It is often awkward, if you are a guest of the Governor—i.e., of the Crown—to get out on your own and freely see nationalist—or even revolutionary—leaders who were vehemently opposing British rule. The British are, however, shrewd about such matters, and most governors leaned over backwards to let us wander around as freely as we chose. What splendidly dedicated men most of these governors were—Arden-Clarke on the Gold Coast; Twining in Tanganyika; Macpherson in Nigeria; Rennie and Kennedy in the Rhodesias; above all, Cohen in Uganda. They differed widely in attainments and temperament, but they knew their jobs and several helped us beyond measure, quite aside from the fact that they achieved the feat of being regal hosts with the utmost informality.

In sharp contrast, most of the American representation

in Africa was at that time indifferent with some honorable exceptions. We Americans were not rulers like the British, of course, and we had no comparable stake. We could not send out ambassadors to more than a fistful of countries, because most of Africa was not yet independent. In some cities we had men of the utmost competence, like John Carter Vincent in Tangier, whose career was later destroyed by vilification during the McCarthy period, but in other watchtowers were staid old horrors. A very bright young man served us in Khartoum (where the British had never permitted us to have any representation at all until a year or two before), and in Tunis we had a consul general who, wonder of wonders, really knew what was going on. Henry Villard was an admirable minister in Libya. But in other seminal posts we had nobody at all, and in several of the big colonial capitals we were served by consuls general about to reach retirement age, some of whom had little talent for politics and knew practically nothing about the steep incandescent rise of African nationalism taking place under their very noses. Indeed, back home the State Department had no true African division at all; Africa was thrown in with the Near East or handled piecemeal, depending mostly on whether the country was French, British, Belgian, or what not. Now this situation is happily changed. The department has a strong African division, with a good many first-class men heading full diplomatic missions out in the field.

Finally, as a result of research in London, I took a day off there and wrote a memorandum listing about *thirty* subjects which I thought would make magazine articles or sections of the book, outlining each briefly. Not all of them turned out to be usable, but at least a dozen did and I checked on every one in the course of our long trip.

III

At last we reached African soil, arriving in Tangier from Madrid. I shall not, in this book which is swelling far beyond its original design, write about our trip. This I have covered fully enough, heaven knows, in *Inside Africa* itself. Sir Ernest Oppenheimer showed us diamonds in Johannesburg; Dr. Albert Schweitzer showed us lepers in Lambaréné. We met potentates with titles as plangent as the Pasha of Marrakesh, the Sultan of Zanzibar, and the Asantehene of Ashanti. His Imperial Majesty Haile Selassie of Ethiopia, a spirited little gnome, granted us an audience, and so did Dr. Kwame Nkrumah, the flashing showboy of the Gold Coast. The public characters I liked best were General Naguib in Egypt, soon to be deposed, and Sylvanus Olympio, who is now President of Togoland. We enjoyed Arab *diffas* (feasts) in North Africa, and a lion brushed the front fender of our car in Kenya. We had one encounter with a cobra in Uganda, and others with white Afrikaner nationalists in the Union almost as virulent.

One of our difficulties—no new thing!—was financial. Canfield and Hamilton had given us sound advances (Hamilton and Roger Machell, his associate, had been pulling hard for an Africa book for a long, long time), but, as usually happens, most of the money was spent long before we started and these were advances *against royalties.* The cost of the trip I had to bear myself. So, just before we left New York, I went to DeWitt Wallace of *Reader's Digest,* and he paid me for three articles in advance. This was agreeable, but it meant that almost as soon as we had seen our first country, Morocco, I had to sit down to write something. During the journey I wrote nine articles in all, which works out to an average of almost one a month. But, for perfectly good reasons, the *Digest* took only one of these, and thus, when I returned to America the next year, I found, embarrassingly enough, that I might be in the awkward position of having to keep on writing for the rest of my life, until the *Digest* liked and accepted two more articles, in order to pay off the rest of its advance. Before I could do any consecutive or sustained work on the book as a whole I had somehow to produce those two *Digest* articles. To my vast relief, the *Digest* took the first two I did—one on uranium in the Congo and the other on medicine murders in Basutoland, and I was free at last to go ahead.

But the book took a very long time indeed to write, and I was forced on several occasions to stop work on it in order to write miscellaneous magazine articles. A vicious circle closed around us. The longer it took me to complete the book, because of these delays, the more did I have to continue writing articles which had nothing to do with Africa at all, and which in turn caused further inevitable delay. The more I worked the further did I find myself from completion of the project. Also I had to fulfill an obligation made years before to do a lecture tour, which ate up six precious weeks. The whole adventure would have ended in ruin if it had not been for continuing co-operation from the *Digest,* which—on top of the original three articles—took no fewer than nine more while the work progressed. Additional chapters were picked up by *Look,* the *American Weekly, Collier's,* the *Saturday Review,* and other magazines.

I wanted to make *Inside Africa* structurally similar to its predecessors and, after an introductory chapter, started off with a personality, the Sultan of Morocco. To hinge a country on a personality is always a risky business and necessitates an intricate organization of material. But I did not *write* the Moroccan chapters until much later. I started writing with Nigeria, the chapters on which appear in the latter part of the book. I wanted to peg out a single country and see how much room it would take. Those trial-run Nigerian chapters had to be rewritten three times. Events were always catching us out, not only in Nigeria but elsewhere; for instance, Nasser replaced Naguib after we left Egypt, and consequently the Egypt I had seen and the Egypt I had to write about were two quite different things. As usual, we had to play with proofs until the last moment of the final hour.

For two consecutive summers we had to move our reference library, which was staggeringly large, from New York to Greensboro, Vermont, and back again. More than once I thought in desperation that the book would *never* be finished. My table of contents kept expanding mercilessly. Exhausted, but continually stimulated too, I would report my progress to friends by saying that I was nineteen forty-thirds finished, then twenty-seven forty-fifths, then thirty-nine forty-sixths. One night in Vermont, with a moon like a lollypop outside my window and insects pleasantly chirping in the garden, I had to face Kenya, and I began to break down my notes. A day of two later it was necessary to confront the printed matter I had collected on Kenya, a multitude of clippings. At least a thousand clippings, as well as a hundred or more long magazine articles, awaited close scrutiny and classification. And do you know what I did? I did not read a single one! I tossed them all back in a trunk! Ever since then I have felt a vestige of bad conscience about this, but the gesture did me good. I felt released.

The most trying circumstance I can remember about any of my books had to do with the conclusion of *Africa.* For various reasons I had decided to write the four South African chapters last. These, it happens, lie directly athwart the middle of the book. We were going to press chapter by chapter. The problem now was that the tightness of the manufacturing schedule became such that all leeway disappeared. The book had to be paginated. We could not go from galley into page proof beyond the middle of the book until the four South African chapters were in type, because of technical difficulties. On June 17, 1955, Canfield sent me a stern memo saying that the first of the four South Africas would have to be delivered on June 20, the second on June 27, the third on July 5, and the fourth on July 8 *by noon*. We were working actually in terms of hours. All this reminded me happily of newspaper days. Another complication was that Harper's had to know in advance the length of the last of the four chapters *within 100 words*. The amiable frenzy attending these weeks was considerable. My wife and I sweated it out all day and worked deep into the night meeting each successive weekly deadline. At the end we counted the words of the last chapter to see if it met the estimate I had previously turned in—3,700 words. The chapter was a shade too long. I pared it to size, but, because of last-minute revision, pared too much. This is why the book, when it came out, had a blank page on 556, I hope not too conspicuous, on the reverse side of a chart.

Adlai Stevenson was taking his first flight to Africa at about that time, and Canfield thought that the book might be useful and had a few special sets of galleys run off for him and his companions on air-mail paper. On ordinary paper the galleys would have presented a problem in overweight. Naturally I was amused by this. (Years later newspaper colleagues told me that no fewer than nine copies of *Inside Russia Today* were to be found on the planes that took Vice-President Nixon and his party to the U.S.S.R.)

IV

Publication of *Africa* came in September, 1955, and the book did nicely although not nearly so well as *U.S.A.* People here simply were not ready to have a thousand pages of smallish type on Africa thrust at them. Hamilton, however, on the British side, did better with it than with any book of mine since *Europe*. Soon translations began to appear—in Arabic and Polish among other languages. Contracts were signed for a Yugoslav edition to be published in Zagreb, but the project did not materialize. When I visited Moscow in 1956 Mr. Gromyko, the Foreign Minister, mentioned casually that he thought *Inside Africa* should be translated into Russian, but so far as I know that was the end of the matter. We went through complex agonies, as usual, in France. The book took a long time to translate, and by the time a draft was ready, much of the book was, Paris said, out of date. Then came further inexplicable delays. Finally the book did appear in French, three years late, under the title *L'Autre Afrique*, but it was something of an astonishment to discover that, without my permission, every line having to do with any French territory in Africa had been ruthlessly cut out.

Africa does not, I believe, exist in Braille, but it has been recorded by Recording for the Blind, Inc. An attempt to make an album out of it (not for the blind) using African drumbeats, animal sounds, and the like, was initiated by Caedmon Records, Inc., but after a good deal of work by me and others the project was abandoned.

The American edition of *Africa* has two jackets, one brown, one green. This is because Jane and I did not like the green chosen by Harper's, and our friend Alexander Liberman, the art director of *Vogue*, did us the service of making some experiments with other colors. The result was a combination of brown, white, and yellow, which we liked so much that Harper's agreed to print half the jackets in their original green version and half in the Liberman variation. Orders from bookstores were divided. The two most unusual printer's bloops I have ever known to occur in a book of mine came in *Inside Africa.* My surprise may be imagined when I saw, reading proof in the fifty-ninth moment of the eleventh hour, a reference to Christ's *"manager."* What I had written was Christ's "manger." In another passage St. John the Baptist came out *"Sir"* John. The jingle that appears at the opening of the book was taken from a slim volume of verse signed "H.B." which was lent me by a British friend; I did not learn until years later that this H.B. was Hilaire Belloc.

We went to Europe the minute proofs were closed, and a month or two later an advance copy of the book reached us in Munich. I spent a solid week reading it. When a book comes out, I try to go through it carefully at once to see what slips the printer may have made, especially if the final passages have been written in a hurry, as they almost always were, and to make corrections of my own errors for the next edition. My first emotion on picking up a new book is always one of trepidation, if not outright terror. After this first reading I seldom, if ever, look at a book of mine again. An acquaintance in New York asked me the other day how I managed to keep so much detail accumulated from all the Insides fresh in my mind. I answered that I didn't—that, on the contrary, a book passed almost completely out of my memory as soon as I had finished it. If anyone should ask me today what is the capital of Gambia I am not at all sure that I would know.

Amiable critics have said that the timing of my books has usually been good, but *Inside Africa* certainly came out too early. Obviously the African "story" was the potent rise of nationalism, the fiercely steep climb of colonial peoples to independence. I concentrated on this as my major theme. Many authorities, some of whom knew a great deal more about parts of Africa than I did, thought that I was stressing nationalism far too much. Actually my error was the opposite. I did not stress it enough. At that time even the most responsible and seasoned British administrators were apt to say, somewhat patronizingly, that "their" people might be ready for national independence in, let us say, 1980. I knew that it was bound to come much sooner than that in several countries, but I never dreamed that it would come as quickly as it did. If anybody had told me in 1953 that Tunisia and Morocco would both be free, independent states within three years, I would have thought he was crazy. Hardly anybody at that time even dreamed of the turbulent evolution whereby the number of independent countries in Africa rose from five to more than thirty in ten short years.

In Africa itself the impact made by *Inside Africa* was considerable. It was interesting to observe how grateful the British were for my opinion that British colonial rule was the best. I do not think that, twenty or thirty years ago, they would have been particularly impressed by any compliments paid their African administration by any outsider, let alone an American journalist. Those who disliked the book most were the Belgians, the Portuguese, and in particular the Liberians. As recently as March, 1961, copies of *Africa* were seized from travelers by the authorities in Mozambique. As to Liberia, it was not forgiven me in Monrovia that I printed such choice items as the fact that the total Liberian appropriation for public health was less than that for brass bands, and that guests at official picnics were greeted by bursts of machine-gun fire—in the air, of course. Furious and prolonged denunciations greeted me in the Liberian press. One indignant attack ended with the words, "The man is a swine!"

Several years ago Edward R. Murrow and Fred Friendly did something nice in connection with their TV show on Africa when they gave the book a credit although none was called for in any way. No matter where their camera teams went on the African continent they found that I had already seen and used what they themselves, reaching the scene, decided that they had to use. Nothing was taken from my book directly, but they felt that they must make some acknowledgment of the manner in which I had anticipated them. The chief virtue of *Inside Africa* is, indeed, the way it explored an important region which at that time was much neglected. No one had ever tried to do what I sought to do—get the whole enormous exploding continent into a single volume. Nor has anybody done so since.

V

In 1956-1958 came *Inside Russia Today*. I had no idea at all of doing a Russian book. In fact I was preparing, in a halfhearted way, for a long trip to Australia, New Zealand, and perhaps Antarctica. These are, so to speak, my "last" continents. Writing about them would, I thought (and still think), complete my so-called "grand design," to do a kind of political guide to the whole of the known world of today.

But in the spring of 1956, or perhaps earlier, Robert Graff of NBC outlined to me an extraordinarily ambitious television project about the Soviet Union. He envisaged a five-month trip in a private aircraft with a staff of a dozen or more; he planned to photograph everything from Kiev to Vladivostok and back again, see everybody, and lay the whole of the U.S.S.R. bare. I was to be narrator or commentator. There followed discussions of detail with NBC and I agreed to go, although I was convinced that the trip, as originally conceived, could not possibly materialize; I did not think the Russians would give sufficient co-operation. Mr. Graff made a "dry run" to Moscow to conclude the arrangements but, as I had feared, the plan eventually collapsed.

News of this became known in New York, and *Collier's* called up one day and said that if I was not going to Russia for NBC would I go for it instead, if I could get a visa. We came to a quick agreement, and, somewhat to my surprise, visas for myself and my wife were soon forthcoming. *Collier's* commissioned us to do five articles. On a parallel assignment was David Douglas Duncan, the photographer, and we worked closely together. We happened to arrive in Moscow immediately before the Hungarian uprising (October, 1956) and the Anglo-French-Israeli attack on Egypt and Suez. Once more I happened by accident to be in a fairly hot place when a war seemed about to begin. I remembered that the Korean War had broken out in 1950 three or four days after Jane and I arrived in Japan, and friends in Moscow greeted us with the taunt that whenever I bobbed to the surface anywhere it was time for the women and children to dive for the nearest bomb shelter.

I should add parenthetically that *Collier's* was shot out from under us during the Russian journey. Irving Levine of NBC broke this news to us, in piquant circumstances, just after we returned from Tiflis on the day before we were to leave Moscow. So I had no magazine to write for. But by the time we arrived in Copenhagen late the next afternoon I had a job again. A cable awaited us with the news that my old friend *Look* had taken over the *Collier's* contract.

VI

Preparations for Russia were almost as exhaustive as for Africa, but somehow proceeded in a lighter vein. First I called on a number of Russian experts in New York, and we accumulated a good many introductions. By chance I met William Benton, publisher of the *Encyclopaedia Britannica* and a former senator from Connecticut, in a restaurant; he had just returned from the Soviet Union and put at my disposal a large folio of memoranda which proved to be of the utmost value. Then Jane and I set out for London, where we spent two strenuous weeks being briefed. London, as a rule, is the best city in the world for such a purpose. The British are highly sophisticated briefers, and catch on at once to what you want.

Before leaving New York I had written about forty letters to Russians in Moscow and elsewhere in the Soviet Union, enclosing a brief biographical statement about myself, explaining my mission, and asking for an appointment. The list was carefully assembled; it included not merely political people but writers, editors, artists, scientists, and so on. Then in London it occurred to me that if a person in New York, say, should get a letter out of the blue from someone in Moscow *in Russian,* he would almost certainly have to go to the considerable nuisance of having it translated. So, attempting to circumvent this language barrier, I had the letters I had sent from New York in English translated *into Russian,* and mailed them again from London. Finally when we reached Moscow I sent out the same letters once more in both English and Russian. This was laborious, but fun.

While we were still in London, I even went to the length of having visiting cards printed in Russian because I wasn't sure we could have this done in Moscow. Of course there is nothing novel in this. Years ago in the Far East—and in Moscow too as a matter of fact on previous trips—I carried cards identifying myself in the local language, as did all the resident American correspondents. Also in London an acquaintance, who had just returned from the Soviet Union, made available to me his private telephone book. I knew that no telephone book existed for the use of visitors or even the general public in Moscow, and I copied out carefully and kept with me a few dozen numbers that I thought might be useful, like those of the American Embassy and Foreign Office. Then, flying into Moscow from Copenhagen, I became alarmed. I had been assured by everybody that the Russians nowadays never even looked at a traveler's baggage at a frontier, much less searched his papers, but I am an old Moscow hand and remembered how, in 1935, I had seen Soviet customs officials riffle through every page of books carried by visitors, and even slit open tubes of toothpaste looking for incriminating material. My little list of telephone numbers might be found; even though it was utterly innocent I might well be interrogated endlessly, or even arrested as a spy. I marched nervously, but with a bold front, to the lavatory on the plane, tore up my hoard of numbers, and deposited the fragments of paper in the toilet. Then —God help us!—I realized that toilets on airplanes do not flush.

To the forty-odd letters we sent to Moscow dignitaries from New York and London I received exactly three written replies. The rest of the letters might as well have been dropped down a manhole. But half a dozen men and women, when we met them later, said that they had indeed received our letters but had not had the "time" to reply. All this preparation paid off. An embassy official told me later that he could recall no American visitor, except possibly Bill Benton, who had managed to see so many Soviet notables on and off the beaten track in so brief a time. Altogether, I saw and took notes of conversations with about eighty Soviet personalities, ranging from the director of the Hermitage Museum in Leningrad to the rector of Moscow University, from members of the Academy of Science to the director of the Puppet Theater in Moscow to a venerable historian in Samarkand, as well as writers, editors, and so forth in profusion. As a counterweight to this I should add that (a) we almost never met a Russian citizen *alone* and (b) only twice did we see the inside of a Russian home.

Several elements contributed to our good luck aside from my own letters and the letters of introduction from friends in America and England which, like billiard balls sent plopping into pockets one by one, we distributed carefully on successive days. One was the fact that I made a good impression on the head of the Intourist Bureau in our hotel. The day after our arrival he told us that he had made the necessary arrangements for us to visit a factory and a nearby collective farm. I took a long chance and said that both factories and collective farms bored me to death and that I did not have the faintest intention of wasting time on them. Puzzled, he asked what I did want to see. I replied, "A first-rate lunatic asylum, the academy where you train artists in Socialist realism, and a musician."

In the entire history of the Soviet Union nobody had ever made such a request. Russians, as always, respond to a challenge. The lunatic asylum, art institute, and musician were magnificently provided for us within forty-eight hours. Second, we were given a particularly good, strong-minded, and intelligent interpreter, Zoya by name, with whom we managed to establish a relationship of trust. She was a fanatically indoctrinated Communist and did not in the least approve of us, but she was impressed by the way we got around. I think that the turning point came on our trip to Alma-Ata in Central Asia, near the border of China. We arrived at Moscow airport at 11:00 P.M. to catch a plane scheduled to depart at midnight, but it did not take off until ten the next morning. We waited up all night, and then had a 24-hour flight in a nonpressurized, nonjet twin-motor ship, with seven or eight stops in the frozen bleakness of Siberia and Kazakhstan. In other words, we spent two nights in a row sitting up without sleep under conditions uncomfortable in the extreme. But an hour after arrival in Alma-Ata we set out to fulfill a crowded schedule of appointments. Jane withstood this ordeal better than I did. From that time on Zoya respected our stamina, if nothing else.

As a matter of fact, I think that she really came to like us; certainly we worked well together. In Leningrad, as an example, I would suggest to her casually that it might be a good idea to have a look at such a seldom visited holy-of-holies as the Pavlov Institute, where the theory of the conditioned reflex was first worked out; without a murmur she would waddle to the telephone, track down the director, and talk him into giving us an appointment, all of this being extraordinary for the Soviet Union. Similarly, without the slightest preparation, we met a bizarre miscellany of characters in Kiev, Sukhumi, Tashkent, Yalta, and elsewhere. I am certain that Zoya had been instructed from above to be as helpful to us as possible and of course was ordered to report on our every step, if necessary; but the personal relationship counted too.

I tried hard to get a political interview with Khrushchev, but ignominiously failed. I did, however, meet him at several diplomatic receptions and exchanged a word or two with him, as well as with other members of the Presidium. In fact, I was standing within ten feet of Mr. K. when he made his celebrated threat to bury the Western nations. Some remarkable events occurred when we sought to have our visas extended; we were very nearly pitched out of the country overnight at the end of our first thirty days, but then managed to get two additional periods of grace. Then, too, I should mention "Operation Anvil." This was the code name for a British manhunt and cleanup drive during the Mau Mau trouble in Kenya. The Soviet Foreign Minister at this time, Dimitri T. Shepilov, mentioned Operation Anvil in a speech at the UN in New York while we were in Moscow, and, to my enormous surprise, quoted me as a source for what had happened. He was attempting to draw analogies between repression by the British in Kenya and events following the Soviet intervention in Hungary, and his speech was printed in full in *Pravda,* including the reference to me. Now, *Pravda* is read with extreme care by everybody who counts in Russia, and the fact that my name had appeared in it made a considerable impression on citizens, particularly in the outlying republics, and helped open several doors to us.

I took an oath during this trip not to write anything while en route, and I adhered to this faithfully. The minute we returned to New York, early in 1957, life began in earnest. Dan Mich of *Look,* with whom I have worked in close harmony for twenty years or more, decided to print one long article—very long—instead of the five that *Collier's* had commissioned; it ran to 14,000 words, and was the longest article *Look* had ever printed as of that date. I wrote it strictly from my notes, using no bibliographical material at all. After a brief holiday in Jamaica I plunged into *Inside Russia Today,* which Harper's and Hamilton were awaiting with impatience. But the book was not to any degree an extension of the *Look* article; I started out totally anew, with a different scale in mind and from a different point of view.

Writing *Russia* took from March, 1957, to February, 1958. I do not think that I have ever had to work with such sustained concentration against various obstacles. One helper was Theodore Shabad, author of a standard work on Russian geography and at present a Moscow correspondent of the *New York Times,* who checked my MS for the correct spelling of Russian words and names. Meantime I had an appalling amount of reading and other research to do. I wanted to cover the whole waterfront and somehow write a book that would contain everything the average reader might want to know about the Soviet Union.

Somewhere in this reminiscence I have mentioned an occasion when I worked all night. Sleepless nights are another matter. I haven't had many, but one certainly occurred in the middle of writing *Russia.* I could not work out the organization. I wrestled with it day after day. I had written some historical and descriptive matter, but this made a bulky and unpleasant bulge in the middle of the book, which I knew must be distributed elsewhere. But how? Where? The offending chapter was tentatively numbered 5A, and I still remember this in troubled dreams.

More than ordinarily I was plagued by the rapid progression of events. Molotov, Malenkov, and Company were ousted from power at the worst possible moment for me—just after I had finished writing about them. Later Zhukov fell. I had to do a good deal of revision, and for this and other reasons found myself months behind schedule. A remarkable bit of luck had to do with the first Sputnik, which was discharged into the heavens on October 4, 1957, after I thought I had written all that was necessary about Russian science, military effort, and the like. The Sputnik made it imperative to alter passages throughout the entire book. But in truth the fact that I was late turned out to be good fortune. Our original publication date had been the very week in October when the Sputnik went up. If I had actually finished the book in time for publication then, it would have had no word in it about the Sputnik just when the world became overwhelmingly Sputnik conscious, and my book would have been dead at birth. The fact that I had been slow in the writing meant that I was able to get the Sputnik material in.

VII

Inside Russia Today finally came out in April, 1958, six months late. Once again we had a Book-of-the-Month Club choice. All seven Insides have been Book-of-the-Month Club selections in one category or other, as well as three of my other books, which means that my debt to my friend Harry Scherman and his staff, as well as to the judges, is literally immeasurable over many years. Immediately after publication *Russia* was widely syndicated; for instance, it appeared in the New York *Herald Tribune* and in the London *Daily Express*, as well as in a multitude of papers on the Continent, even though the original *Look* article also had been widely sold abroad, for example to the *Sunday Times* in London. Also the *Reader's Digest* printed several chapters. Then came a few translations. Gallimard dropped me and the French rights went to Hachette. A contract was signed and an advance paid, but even so the French translation has never appeared. I inquired about this in Paris in 1960, more than two years after American publication. The Hachette executives told me vaguely that it had taken them so long to translate the book that they would probably not publish it at all. Obviously my luck with France continues to be bad. The Italian edition, published by Garzanti in Milan, is the handsomest translation I have ever seen of my book in a foreign language. The Chinese pirates on Taiwan picked up *Russia* in their jolly way, and one new language came to the Insides with this book —Hebrew. The Japanese edition, a luxurious production, embarrassed me slightly because the cover of one volume is adorned with a photograph of Mr. Khrushchev, the other with one of me. A paperback edition in Braille (15 volumes) soon appeared, and the book has been recorded as well in the Talking Books program of the Library of Congress (16 disks) and is available on magnetic tape (9 reels) as recorded by the American Foundation for the Blind, Inc.

I was naturally curious about the reception both the *Look* article and the book would get in Russia itself, if any. The Soviet press blew both hot and cold. The book received four major reviews, including one in *Pravda*—something unusual and probably unprecedented, since it was not translated into Russian, did not appear there, and could not conceivably have been bought in a Soviet bookstore. For reviews to appear at all (one was even picked up by an American wire service and cabled back to the United States) was thus exceptional. As may be imagined, the book was denounced and castigated by Russian critics, but the denunciations were respectful on the whole; even official apologists for the Soviet regime had to concede that I was trying to be fair. But this was among the things that bothered them most. It was inconceivable to them that an observer could, on the one hand, say that Soviet rulers sometimes behaved like didactic hobgoblins and, on the other, commend highly their achievements in such fields as science, industry, and education. For Russians everything has to be one way or the other, black or white.

Even though *Russia* has not been translated into Russian, it is quite widely known in the U.S.S.R. Hundreds upon hundreds of American, British, and Western European officials or tourists, using it as a Baedeker, brought copies in with them, and then gave these to Russian friends or acquaintances. This process still goes on. The books are passed around from hand to hand, and eventually leak out to the public at large. About a year ago a copy of the book was bringing 100 rubles ($10) in the Moscow black market, which almost puts me on the same level as a Sinatra record.

I have often been asked why "Today" appears in the title. This was a matter of fierce dispute between Canfield, my wife, and myself. My chief motives were to vary the pattern of the other Inside titles, and indicate that the book dealt with a Russia vastly changed from that which I had seen and written about before the war.

VIII

One day early in 1960 Hobart Lewis of *Reader's Digest* asked me if I had ever heard of a book called *Inside Europe* and if I remembered when it had been published. He chuckled when, after thinking a moment, I replied in an aghast voice that I had started work on it exactly twenty-five years before. Mr. Lewis proceeded to suggest that I should set out on a brief European journey and write for the *Digest* an article comparing the Europe of today with that of 1935, a quarter of a century ago. This invitation was irresistible and, shelving Australia once more, Jane and I took off for London, Paris, Berlin, and Rome. The trip was brief, but the aftermath arduous. Returning to America, I started to write, and could not stop because I wanted to do a book as well as the *Digest* piece. Before the summer was over I turned in to the *Digest* material which ran to 42,000 words—the longest "article" it has ever received. This embarrassed Mr. Lewis greatly. I had violated one of the most important of all canons covering work of this kind. By overwriting enormously I vastly exceeded the terms of our agreement and put up to him a problem—cutting—which should have been solved by me. To a good editor, a writer who overwrites is almost as menacing as one who underwrites. But Mr. Lewis braced himself to the shock and in the end the *Digest* made three articles out of my fat, unwieldy mass of manuscript.

For years Canfield and Hamilton had been urging upon me the possibility of revising the original *Inside Europe*. From year to year I evaded the suggestion. Now I told them that they could, if they wished, use the 42,000-word *Digest* material as a "pamphlet." I was overruled. They insisted on something longer, and in the end I promised to expand what I had written into a short book running to 60,000 or 70,000 words. I started work and of course soon discovered that I had to tackle the project from a different angle. So, laboriously, I started all over again and set out to do a full-dress book, which we decided to call *Inside Europe Today*. Eventually it reached a perfectly respectable length, although it is the shortest of all the Insides, and it was duly published in August, 1961, after a year of intermittent struggle. A revised edition followed in April, 1962, appearing in both hard cover and paperback (Pocket Books, Inc.). By this time several of my older books were coming out in paperbacks, but this was the first big paperback sale I ever had.

Going through my files recently I discovered two things which I had completely forgotten and which astonished me. In my own particular sieve of memory some apertures are large. I found that back in 1945 I had written a letter to Hamilton registering *Inside Europe Now* as a title and that, when the *Herald Tribune* serialized *Behind the Curtain* in 1949, it used the title *Inside Europe Today*. If anybody had told me this I would not have believed it. I thought *Inside Europe Today* was a brand-new title. But the fact that I had apparently been thinking in terms of revising *Europe* fifteen years before I did so is another indication of the continuity of purpose, the unity of design, that I have mysteriously felt during most of my writing life. Nothing can be more useful to a writer than a sense of inner architecture.

As I look back now at all seven Insides my chief feeling is that, though I did not work nearly as hard on them as most people assume, the sustained concentration of effort they required *while* I was writing took a large toll out of me, no matter how much fun the process was. But—I hasten to add—the rewards for this endeavor have been handsome, materially and otherwise, and I have no complaints. I have met some interesting people, and my name is widely known. What I am about to put down should not be put down by me, but let me pamper myself. Once a British journal, preposterously but agreeably, called me "Surveyor-General to the Universe," and when we arrived in Tanganyika the Governor, Sir Edward Twining, now Lord Twining, assembled his chief advisers and told them that he regarded a visit by me as the equivalent of one from a Royal Commission. As far back as 1952 Charles Poore of the *New York Times,* reviewing one of my books, coined the word "guntherize" with a small "g." This usage has become fairly common. A *Harper's* reviewer once called Chester Wilmot's book on Europe a "guntherian symphony," and recently I came across a line in the *New York Times* to the effect that something ought to be "re-guntherized." *Time* has also used this coinage. I must admit that I had never thought to see myself in lower case.

CHAPTER V

Inside the Insides

When jack fischer asked me to write this reminiscence he suggested that I give particular stress to concrete details of my methods of work, both while out in the field and at home. What he wanted was, in a word, a trade secret or two. It seems to me that the first essence of journalism is to *know what you want to know;* the second, to find out who will tell you. My friend the late Walter Duranty made a joke about a colleague once: "He thinks with his ears." I don't know whether I myself actually think with my ears, but I certainly try to use them. Another rule on a quite different level is: *Never take notes on both sides of the same sheet of paper.*

I hate to strike a country altogether cold. A visitor should know in advance what the chief background issues are; hence a bit of reading can be profitable, quite aside from briefing by word of mouth. On the other hand, it is also important *not to know too much*—there is such a thing as being too familiar with a subject, in which case you lose freshness and the capacity for surprise. Most of my preliminary reading is in the form of newspaper and magazine clippings. I do not read much in books as a rule until the trip is done or sometimes not until I have finished writing about a subject—probably because I don't want to be influenced—but even so my reading is extensive—as may be seen, for instance, by the fact that the *Africa* bibliography contains 275 titles. Our *U.S.A.* library is even larger.

Clippings come mostly from a kind of morgue I have kept for more than thirty years. I glance at a wide variety of American and British newspapers and magazines, mark them, and have them clipped and filed. I have never counted, but I must have several hundred thousand clippings in all. Until recently they lay in a basement on East 62nd Street. Maintaining this morgue became a hobby. For years I did the actual clipping and filing myself. It is incomprehensible to me now how I happened to start this process, and I am startled half out of my skin from time to time by discovering some unexpected treasure. When I began work on *Inside U.S.A.* I found that I had clippings from the London *Times* and other European newspapers marked and meticulously ticketed, "North Carolina—Labor" or "Mormons—Social Patterns" dating back to 1925. I don't say that all these old bits of paper were useful. But I continue to be astonished that, back in the neolithic past of the middle twenties, I was systematically assembling material for books that I had no idea I would ever write, in a pattern that did not even begin to become clear until *Inside Europe* ten years later.

Similarly, when I set out for Africa I found that I had preserved old articles from the *New York Times* or the *Economist* or what not on subjects ranging from the economy of Togoland to tribal customs on the Nile. And when assembling material for *Inside Russia* I found folders filled with clippings which went back three decades, including early glimpses of the Russian Revolution by authors who subsequently became well known, which were still extraordinarily fresh and revealing. Again I ask myself what strange, cryptic impulse made me file away all this material so many years ago. The answer is that I do not know.

II

Next comes the brutal step of planning an itinerary. I have already alluded to some of our adventures in logistics. The business of hiring a car for a trip to the Congo can kill a day. The principal problem is the careful allotment of time. Take *Latin America.* I had twenty-nine cities to visit in twenty countries and I had to work out at least tentatively how much time I would spend in each. Or take Africa, a continent where, as I once wrote, airplanes run every other Tuesday. Should Cairo get fifteen days and Addis Ababa eleven? If I had to choose between the Ivory Coast and the Cameroons, which should I pick? In those days a traveler would often have to decide between spending two days in a certain city, not enough, or ten, too much, because of crazily haphazard communications. The first law of travel was instantly on arrival in a town to lay down lines for getting out.

No matter how carefully we plotted our arrangements, we could not fix a complete itinerary months ahead. It was necessary to leave loopholes. I must say, though, that in general we kept pretty closely to schedule. This was essential, because we sought above all to hold fast to a terminal date previously set. Otherwise the temptation would have been to stretch every trip by months. Let me tell a small anecdote having to do with *U.S.A.* I was having a splendid time in Rhode Island, a state I had never visited before. Then it dawned on me that if I gave ten days or two weeks to the smallest state, what would I do with the giant mass of Texas? what with California? I proceeded to get out of Rhode Island at once, and swore to myself that I would not return. Rhode Island was finished, done with, for good and all, forever. Some time later I had lunch with the late Robert E. Sherwood. He was writing *Roosevelt and Hopkins,* but, after months of strenuous effort, he had not been able to get beyond Hopkins' youth—he was still miles away from F.D.R. himself. I told him my Rhode Island story. Mr. Sherwood scowled with attention and, as a result, determined then and there to cut off mercilessly all further work on the early Hopkins and plunge at once into the real body of his book. For years we had this little episode between us, and I suppose he must have mentioned it to me later at least twenty times.

Sometimes travel plans are beyond the writer's control. I tried hard to get a Soviet visa several times between 1947 and 1956, but never succeeded. In those days the Russians, after demanding that you produce an autobiography and putting you through various other laborious procedures, seldom—if ever—formally rejected an application for a visa. All that happened was that you never got it. No word, yes or no, ever came. Once, though, I gained a considerable amount of prestige by being actually *refused* a visa—unprecedented honor! This came about because an American soldier of marked eminence, who was then the president of a university, did me the favor of communicating with the American Ambassador in Moscow at the time, a military man, suggesting that he intervene with the Russian authorities in my behalf. His thought was that a book on Russia by me would be valuable reading for Americans. Five months later I duly received a reply—to the effect that Mr. Vishinsky, the Soviet Foreign Minister of the day, did not think that a visit to the U.S.S.R. by me would be "opportune." This was in 1948, and the visa did not finally come through until 1956.

My wife and I are trying to get visas for Red China now. The applications went in three years ago, since when silence from Peking has been frigid and complete.

III

Next, note taking. Notes are the precious raw material out of which books are made. On each trip I assembled a considerable amount of printed documentary matter as well, and we always bought books and pamphlets freely. How to ship all this cargo home safely, in particular the precious, irreplaceable longhand notes, became a serious problem, which we solved in a variety of ways. Some of it we kept with us, and toward the end of the Africa trip, as an example, our overweight charge on baggage was equal to a fare. I have always been a phenomenally heavy—as well as nervous—traveler.

I have never used a tape recorder or other mechanical device. I write notes longhand on small scratch pads, which is not a very scientific method. The ideal is to be able to take notes during the actual course of a conversation, but sometimes this is not possible. There are people who dry up at the sight of a pencil. Moreover, we always do a lot of newsgathering at parties—lunches, dinners, what not—and it really is impossible to take notes during a formal dinner party. So I would try to brace myself to remember what went on, and then, at all costs, scribble a few key words as reminders before we went to bed. Jane is much better at this than I.

Once at a party in Tokyo I was so fascinated by something complicated told me by our host that I excused myself after coffee and went calmly to the powder room where I managed to put the gist of it down on the back of an envelope. If you do not take notes soon after a talk you are in trouble. If, for instance, in Khartoum or Rome or Milwaukee, you see in the course of a day eight or ten people who represent every possible shade of political opinion, it will be virtually impossible to separate one set from another if you wait till nightfall to write them down. Or you may be too tired to remember anything at all. Sometimes, while interviewing somebody not particularly interesting, I have even caught myself jotting down notes from the conversation of somebody I had seen previously, while pretending to be recording the talk of the man I was with. "Yes, yes," I have been known to mutter to Mr. X, "how interesting!" while scribbling down secretly the words of Mr. Y.

I wish I had a better memory and that all this hocus-pocus wasn't necessary. But, just as I can think only with my fingers while actually at a typewriter, I cannot remember anything accurately unless I write it down.

My habit of note taking goes back many years. In the early 1930's I began filing not merely newspaper clippings but notes on conversations. Even when I had no idea whether the notes would ever turn out to be useful, taking them and tucking them away in my morgue envelopes became an amusement. Two episodes come to mind. In 1943, when I was covering the war in Sicily, a British colleague started one night to reminisce eloquently about Africa. His name was Hastings, and he had had considerable experience of that continent. Next day, before we went off to see whatever battle the Germans were being considerate enough to set up for us, I squeezed an hour free and wrote out in longhand the gist of what Mr. Hastings had told me, which covered everything from the name of the best hotel in Durban to the origin of the word "Bantu." I utterly forgot these notes until I came across them in one of my Africa envelopes nine years later, when they proved to be invaluable. Similarly, in 1947, I spent a long weekend with Sinclair Lewis in Massachusetts. He was urging me to start the African trip at once: "Before you get any older." Then he went into one of his stupendous cycles of improvisation and, although he had no real knowledge of Africa, sang out a positive litany of African themes, ideas, and challenges. He composed right out of the blue the plot for a play about Africa and developed all the characters. I wrote down the gist of Lewis' talk before bed that night, and then completely forgot it. But there the notes were waiting in my dossiers when we began our trip in 1952, and they were not only amusing but provocative as well.

I will tell another story parenthetically. Back in 1939 I sat for an hour or two at the Café des Deux Magots in Paris with a girl who had just had a brief trip through the five Central American republics and who was perspicacious about the differences between Guatemala, Costa Rica, and the rest. I suppose I knew at that time that I would go to Latin America someday, but when I returned to my hotel that night and spent half an hour jotting down notes on what Mrs. X had told me I honestly was not doing it with any sense of future utilitarian use, but for fun; my curiosity had been aroused and I wanted to preserve what I had heard for my own enlightenment.

I don't want this to sound didactic, but I have picked up some minor theories about note taking. One is never, never, never, to ask a man his own first name, initials, job, or title. This the interviewer should know beforehand. Again, it is moderately important to define just what "off the record" means. There are plenty of public figures who are disappointed if the interviewer, in an effort to protect *them,* volunteers that the talk will be off the record, because they want to be quoted but hate to admit it. One thing I have found out is that almost any person will talk freely—such is human frailty—if you ask him the measure of his own accomplishment. One effective question is to ask a man what he believes in most; I have collected an interesting anthology of answers to this. In general, if a person is superior, he will enjoy being talked up to or argued with, although the danger exists of letting an interview degenerate into a conversation. The job of an interviewer is to get information, not to show himself off. Just the same, there is no better way to get a spark off some dignitary than to disagree with him, if you are sure of your own ground. If a man evades, try to show him that you know something of his own subject, even if it isn't much. Finally, I have found that the last two or three minutes of an interview are the best. Your victim is so glad that the ordeal is almost over that he loosens up.

As I look back I think that the late Senator Arthur Vandenberg of Michigan was probably the most satisfactory person to interview I ever met. He was lucid, brief, sympathetic, and full of hard facts. Another was the late Josephus Daniels, Wilson's Secretary of the Navy and, much later, F.D.R.'s Ambassador to Mexico. When I met him in Raleigh, North Carolina, he said before I had so much as opened my mouth, "So you want to know who runs North Carolina!" He then proceeded to tell me—with the utmost precision, balance, and comprehensiveness. Among non-Americans, splendid people to interview whom I have seen recently were Willy Brandt, the mayor of West Berlin, and Iain MacLeod, the new leader of the

Conservative Party in England who may well succeed Mr. Macmillan as prime minister. One of the most difficult men to interview (in my experience) is General Charles de Gaulle. Another was Leon Trotsky, but perhaps he was so hard to draw out because he insisted on speaking English, a language which he did not fully command, instead of using an interpreter. Most difficult of all were Moslem potentates whom we met in Africa, like King Idris of Libya and the late Emir of Kano. They were perfectly agreeable but totally unprepared for the kind of questions contemporary journalists ask—also inarticulate through shyness. On the other hand, as delightful and free a talk as any I ever had was with Abdel Krim, the old Riffian chieftain who waged blazing war against France and Spain in the 1920's, and whom we met in Cairo. He is an exceptionally sophisticated personage. I was astonished that he was still alive.

Group meetings, besides being great fun, can be immensely valuable. In Houston, Bogotá, Columbus, Moscow, Tiflis, Cleveland, Cape Town, friends assembled groups for me to meet. It is marvelous when you can get knowledgeable individuals to talk against each other. Throw in some simple question like "What are the chief issues here?" and hope strenuously for acute disagreement—then enlightenment really comes. The walls will shake. Of course, much depends on the mood of the interviewer, particularly his state of exhilaration or fatigue. I remember two or three people whom I had looked forward to meeting for months, and with whom I wanted to be at my best; I was a miserable failure each time—both too eager and too tired to get off the ground. Above all, I would repeat to anybody interested in journalism, "Write it down!" I have just been skimming through some notes I made fifteen years ago. One says, "Silliman Evans and the other J.G." and another is, "For goodness' sake don't forget that Duranty story about the nickel mine." Also I have a note scribbled down in 1944: "Senator Truman on other Senators—most valuable—do this right away." Today I haven't the faintest idea what it was that Evans, Duranty, and Mr. Truman told me. Memory is an unreliable guide at best. So—write down at once what you want to remember and write it down *in full.*

I always did my best to see people on both sides. In America my ideal day was to spend the morning with the Republican National Committee and the afternoon with the Democratic National Committee, to lunch with the CIO and dine with the First National Bank. This can lead to difficulties, because there is nothing more disconcerting than to talk on the same day to two well-informed people in Miami, say, who contradict each other flatly, even on simple questions of fact like who owns the local gasworks. But half the excitement of journalism is the weighing of one source of information against another.

After a trip comes the terrifying moment when, home at last, you open the envelopes of notes that you have carefully shipped ahead. Are any missing? Are they decipherable? Do they still hold value? What follows is laborious. I clip everything apart—which is why notes should never be taken on both sides of the paper—into thousands of little sniplets and subdivide them carefully, covering a card table or two. For a chapter on the Sudan, as an example, I will assemble thirty, forty, fifty small piles of scissored longhand scraps—broken down into Nile, politics, history, Gezira project, Khartoum, personalities, Gordon College, relations with Egypt, British attitudes, civil service, animals, Fuzzy-Wuzzies, what not. One pile is always "Not-Using" and another is "Future Reference," which are likely to turn out to mean the same thing. Another is "Sources." In cutting the original notes apart I try to make a notation on each of who told me what. All this is tiresome. I have come near to yelling aloud in desperation when, having finished eviscerating one notebook, then another, then another, I find that there are still odd bits of paper to lay into fruitful formation. But somebody, I think Logan Pearsall Smith, once said that the true test of a person's love for his vocation was his capacity to tolerate the drudgery it involved. And I suppose that I am a pedant at heart. It is all very mysterious. I wrote a children's "encyclopedia" at eleven (three of its five sections were "Battleships of the World," "Greek Gods and Heroes, with Genealogical Charts," and "Memorable Dates"), and in my high school zoology class I set out to list every species of animal in the world.

At last, when work on the notes is finished, when sources have been checked and essential reading has been done, it is time to write.

IV

Mostly I slog everything out on a typewriter, triple space. I have never been able to get beyond using one finger and my typing is fantastically illiterate partly because I cannot spell. Sometimes when I am having trouble with a chapter I write a few pages in longhand, because this demands more concentration, at least from me. Unfortunately the longhand is all but illegible. I have tried to dictate, but have never mastered the art. There are, however, a few dictated passages in *Inside Russia Today,* and more in the new *Europe*.

At about the time I was doing *Africa* my writing habits at last became organized, some twenty or thirty years late. I work in a pleasant room full of books in

Manhattan or in my ramshackle, delicious hut in Vermont. I sleep late as a rule, and seldom am posted at my desk, which is offensively littered, until around eleven in the morning. One secret of survival, while writing, is to skip lunch—social or business lunches or lunches out. I take time out for a brief bite in the kitchen, but otherwise, at least in theory, try to work straight through till three-thirty or four in the afternoon. Then I have tea and take a nap. At six people usually drop in for a drink or we go out to some party or other. If I am working against a deadline (self-imposed), as I often am, or have achieved a really nice saturation, I work after dinner too. Toward the end of every book it has been essential for me to work at night, which is hard on one's family. To get the last passages of a book done I need two substantial work periods a day, seven days a week.

The key to sustained writing is concentration, saturation, and the trick is to *get your subconscious to work for you.* I write while I sleep. The hard job is to build up the charge that carries you through. Once an illustrious writer, engaged busily on an article, mentioned to me casually, but with astonishment, that she had become so excited about her project that she found herself writing down notes and phrases wherever she went—in taxis, on menus at lunches, and so on. I listened with incredulity. Any time I am well along on a book I do the same thing, and have done so for many years. It astounded me that she had never had this experience before. If, while working, I do not reach out for odd bits of paper several times a day, no matter where I am, and scribble on them I know that my work is not going well. Usually, too, I keep a pad on the bed table. The most germinal of all creative periods is, in my experience, the hour at night that comes *after* a spurt of work is finished. I have a drink or two, and, although the chore of writing is done for the day, the brain is still alive. There can then occur a kind of spontaneous liberation, a foaming overflow, which I strive to put down in disjointed notes.

Another important factor is pace. For me the way to achieve pace is to cut, cut, cut. In the most extraordinary way, which I cannot explain, part of what you cut from a book stays with it. Of course, there can be such a thing as too much cutting; this rubs the bloom off. Also paragraphing is of the utmost importance. Sometimes it is effective to combine two different themes in the same paragraph; I know no device better calculated to keep the reader's nose to the page. Punctuation counts for a good deal as well. My favorite punctuation mark is the semicolon; it gives the reader a bit of breath, but does not destroy continuity. My favorite words are adjectives. One device is to put adjectives together in an unexpected sequence. For instance, say about somebody that he is "a coarse, brilliant man." But the effect of this is ruined if you insert an "and" or a "but" between "coarse" and "brilliant." Even the most insignificant words or phrases can assist or destroy cadence and euphony. There can be a vast difference between "et cetera" and "and so forth" at the end of a sentence.

I never write a book in sequence. This may seem odd, but there is a reason behind it. I like to do a trial run, to pick out a chapter almost at random and write it as a test of length and mood. I have already mentioned that I began the writing of *Africa* with Nigeria, in the middle of the book. This can lead to difficulties, but the experience is valuable because it gives proportion. When I finished the first draft of Nigeria I found to my dismay that I had written almost 20,000 words. Certainly, at that time, Nigeria was a less vital subject than Egypt or South Africa. Yet here I was with 20,000 words. Nigeria was then, and still is, one of about forty African countries. If I dealt with them all on the same scale, my book was obviously going to be longer than the Encyclopaedia Britannica and would take me until the year 2000 to complete. So, much chastened, I pared Nigeria to the bone and proceeded to adjacent realms.

Again, writing chapters out of sequence is useful because it helps to peg out the whole route. It may seem idiotic to begin with Chapter 17, then go back to 5, jump ahead to 33, and return to 9, but this provides landmarks. I have always found it easier to think in terms of filling gaps than of proceeding straight ahead. After doing a few scattered chapters I usually write the last chapter, then the first. One reason why I like to do the *last* chapter early is that it compels me to organize my material carefully and know with certainty what line I will be taking throughout the entire book; another is that it is written while I am comparatively fresh. So many books falter or fail toward the end. Of course, such an idiosyncratic system can cause appalling complications. I must always seek to keep in mind the context of each chapter, the flow of the book as a whole. I have even played little tricks with myself, and in Chapter 14, say, I will write in reference to something, "as has just been noted in Chapter 12 above . . ." although Chapter 12 is not yet written.

I write almost everything, if I have time, three times. This is a curse. I fiddle and faddle. It is my ill fortune never to be able to write a good first draft; I happen, alas, to be one of those luckless creatures who can never get anything right on the initial attempt. First I do an insanely hurried rough draft. I can typewrite ten pages, say 2,000 words, in about three hours. Then this must be revised—often rewritten. My experience is that revision takes just as long as the original writing, perhaps longer.

If it takes me three hours to write a section of a chapter, it will take me three hours or more to revise it. Sometimes hardly a word of the original script survives. Then my good friend and secretary, Alice Furlaud, makes a clean copy of the original typed manuscript with its multitudinous longhand corrections; I go over this again, revising it carefully once more. This draft is, if we have time, typed a third time, and again I scrutinize it. Even if draft No. 3 does not need so much work as No. 2, there are usually a dozen cuts and changes on every page, mostly to amend verbal infelicities. I can never leave a manuscript alone. Draft No. 3, finally corrected, is what goes to the printer. But then I do a good deal of work on proofs—almost enough to warrant the galley proofs being called draft No. 4. A book never seems recognizable to me as such until it is in type; Canfield says, not altogether with approval, that I am the most expensive writer he has ever had to work with. After galley proofs I usually say quits. Either the book is being published so quickly that there is no time for page proofs or I am so stale on the project that I never want to look at it again. I don't know anything in the world as nerve-racking as the finality of proofs. Once or twice I have penciled in final changes while actually in a taxi en route to Harper's.

But this is not quite all. Somewhere along the line comes checking. As I work through the first and second drafts I make jottings on sheets of paper marked "Check," "Permissions," "Quotes," "Sources," "Libel," "Map," "Chart," and "Index." Usually the "Check" pages will contain forty or fifty items per chapter, mostly in the realm of how to spell Awolowo or is such-and-such a date correct. On the "Map" sheet I write down place names which the cartographer may miss; on the "Index" sheet, items which I hope the indexer will not neglect. The

67

Never before had I taken a project so seriously, although I know now that I did not take it seriously enough; my activity was always subject to indulgences and interrupted by bouts of confusion or apathy. One thing making for difficulty was the the national traffic jam caused by the war. I wrote to hotels in every city I intended to visit months in advance (in those days hotels would not accept guests for longer than five days), and inflicted on my secretary, Nancy Barnett — who, incidentally, typed the whole of Inside U.S.A. twice and parts of it three and four times — a ghastly lot of nuisance over similar matters. We wrote to every airline in the United States, to stave off the danger of being bumped, and dealt with other problems in logistics. Gasoline rationing was of course still in force, and travel by automobile was difficult, although on several laps the local authorities shoved me from one

When I go into longhand, which happens more frequently nowadays than before, everybody has trouble. This is a page from Chapter Two of the original manuscript of the present book.

116 B

arisen any number of proposals for amelioiration of the German

problem, attempts to find some sort of solution. These range

from the peculiar catch-all named "disengagement"

which in one form or other is supported by substantial left-wing

sentiment in England and elsewhere, to the Rapacki Plan,

Meantime currents within Germany itself are susceptible of

change. I have stressed in earlier passages of this book Chancellor

Adenauer's devotion to European unity, and, in particular,

Franco-German rapprochment, as well as his spitfired , unequivocal

hostility to the Soviet Union. But the harsh pressures of time

and circumstance

First draft into second. A passage from *Inside Europe Today,* showing original typewritten draft with my long-hand corrections.

reason is
~~many~~ interlocking factors, the main ~~elements of the~~
simple
~~story are clear~~ enough. Given the background, Khrush-
have seemed to
chev's behavior was not as irrational as it may ~~seem~~
M. K. wrecked the Summit because of the
~~to~~ be. ~~The main element was, beyond doubt, violent~~
~~personal outrage over the~~ U-2 affair. It is quite
possible, as several commentators have pointed out,
that the Summit Conference would have been
a failure even if it had taken place because of a
misunderstanding between Khrushchev and Eisenhower
as to exactly what had taken place at Camp David in
but it certainly would have met
reference to Berlin, ~~A good many seasoned folk thought~~
if the U-2 had not made its overflight. The U-2
~~immediately after the Summit, that Khrushchev, having~~
~~made it convenient for~~ The Russian Premier
~~become aware that he was not going to be given any~~
had ~~already~~
~~great concessions about Berlin, determined to blow up~~
~~the conference before May 1, and used the U-2 incident~~
~~as a pretext. But, in the light of what we know, this~~
~~hypothesis simply will not hold water. Khrushchev~~
a convenient pretext for
behaving as he did, but it was much more
than a mere pretext. Khrushchev destroyed

Second draft into third. Another passage from *Inside Europe Today,* illustrating further longhand changes. This is what went to my publisher.

22-B

dering in advance if my allotment of time for Minnesota, say, was not too little, or for South Dakota not too much.

I did little writing while I was actually en route except, of all things, a long article far off my track on the sharp deterioration then beginning (early 1945) in relations between the United States and Russia. This had nothing whatever to do with my book, but my disappointment and apprehension were so acute that I ~~wanted~~ to express myself. My line was that, if Washington and Moscow did not succeed in making a real peace, Hitler—even in death—would turn out to have won the war. Writing this article ruined a week in New Orleans, but I felt better when I had delivered myself of it.

It was interesting, as the U.S.A. trip continued, to see how my reception differed from that which I had had in Europe, Asia, and Latin America. I found that Americans were more accessible than Europeans, more sophisticated in regard to the inquiries of journalism, and prouder of their communities. Most Americans are ~~houseproud. Of course, different sections of the country~~ had their own different patterns. It is certainly a minor criterion, but I was fascinated by the fact that, if my recollection is correct, I was never once interviewed by any local newspaper in New England, ~~the Atlantic seaboard,~~ New York, Pennsylvania, or Southern California. But I was widely sought after and written about all over the Middle West, the mountain states, the South (where I was front-page news in almost every city) and, in particular, Texas. I was even invited to address a joint session of the Texas legislature!

I had no idea how well known I was, unbecoming as it is for me to say this myself, until this journey. Several times people said pleasant things. One was Dr. Douglas

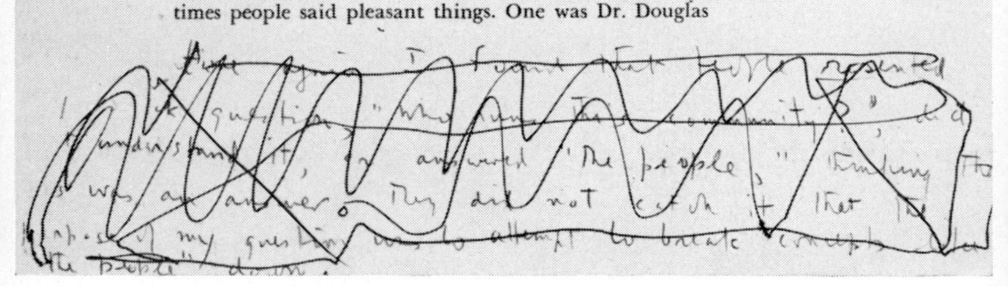

Sometimes galleys become a fourth draft. This sample is from the present book.

worst job, and the one I like best, is "Sources." I try to acknowledge major quotations in footnotes as the book proceeds, but I like to list subordinate sources separately as well. Hence the long sections of notes and acknowledgments at the end of *Inside U.S.A., Inside Africa,* and *Inside Russia Today*—also *Roosevelt in Retrospect.*

One inconvenience throughout all this is that we are always in such a hurry. I am in constant terror that somebody in my dramatis personae will die off. I remember taking time out to read Irwin Shaw's "Tip on a Dead Jockey" in *The New Yorker* one Sunday morning when I was on the last desperate stages of a book, and that I should have given up an hour to this pleasure made me feel like a thief. Similarly I have felt guilt when I have crawled out and sneaked into a movie late on a tortured afternoon. Tortured? Well, not quite! Even the worst moments have, for me, always been enlivened and refreshed by the fact that they were inextricably associated with the creative process, the best thing in life.

One problem has been how to keep abreast of new material. To a certain extent I did this by correspondence, and convenient windfalls sometimes came in the shape of visitors to New York. But mostly my technique, not very satisfactory, was to read various local publications. For instance, while writing *Asia* I relied on the *Hindu* (Madras), the *Japan Advertiser,* and the *China Weekly Review,* to each of which I subscribed for a period. Similarly, while struggling with *U.S.A.,* my secretary went to Times Square once a week and picked up the local newspapers from Atlanta, Louisville, San Francisco, St. Louis, and half a dozen other cities. Perhaps one may think that local developments in the United States are covered adequately in the New York press, but this is not so.

For *Russia* I used mostly the *Current Digest of the Soviet Press,* but as a matter of fact the Soviet Union is better covered in American newspapers than are many American states. I always clip the *New York Times,* the *New Statesman,* et cetera, while a work is in progress and usually, at the very end, I have to face a huge, complicated mass of notes and clippings supplementary to those which I used for the actual book, classified under rubrics like "Since Writing" and "Watch in Proof," which I must laboriously break down, check, and use.

Perhaps the reader will ask what, in the last analysis, determines *what* I write. I try to report facts as I see them and to tell the truth, but truth is an elusive concept. I think it was Frank Lloyd Wright who once said, "The truth is more important than the facts." I would hesitate to recommend this maxim unreservedly to a school of journalism, but surely what Mr. Wright meant is clear—that selection of facts can be as important as the facts themselves. No man, not even Christopher Isherwood, is a camera—and the camera, as a matter of fact, is one of the greatest liars of our time. There is no such thing as *purely* objective journalism, although plenty of us try to get close. A reporter with no bias at all would be a vegetable. I myself have always had a strong, unalterable liberal bent; I believe in decency and progress, in tomorrow as against yesterday. But I am not often swayed or shaken by events. I have little messianic blood in my veins, and I seldom editorialize. On most issues I take a somewhat detached, even cold, old-fashioned middle view, although I stand more to the left than to the right. *Why* do I write? I suppose the best answer to this is that basically I write for myself, to satisfy my own multiple curiosities. In other words, my work has been a kind of exercise in self-education at the public's expense. I myself am a fairly good average guinea pig, and if something interests me I am reasonably sure it will interest the general reader too. I can only hope that the public has had its money's worth.

My colleague the late Raymond Clapper once said, "Never underestimate a reader's intelligence; never overestimate what he knows." I always try to be readable (and readability, to repeat, depends on pace and euphony) and I greatly enjoy making lists and summaries in my attempts to synthesize large masses of material, but I want to be solid as well and I do not believe in being too simple. It is a good thing to make the reader reach up. On the other hand, he has an absolute right to have terms defined; I try hard never to use a word or a phrase, from "apartheid" to "Common Market," without doing my best to explain exactly what it means.

V

And so, at sixty, I have twenty-five years, a quarter century, of Inside books behind me. I have never ceased being astonished that the seven have done so well. I have received far more praise than I deserve. All I can say further is that I hope keenly to do some more. Hardly a month passes without a suggestion from somebody for a new trip. *Inside Canada* is one idea, and a report on the UN another. My book on Washington is still not done, several friends strenuously urge me to attack the Middle East, and I myself continue steadily to accumulate notes, fuss with maps, and work out itineraries for *Inside Australasia.* Already I have written half a dozen tentative outlines for the Australia book, to which I feel committed if I return safely from a projected sojourn in another field which I hope to enjoy soon. Meantime, the old joke turns out to be applicable. In this reminiscence, which I didn't think would occupy more than a score or two of pages, my Insides certainly have been coming out.

Appendix

The following is a memorandum about *Inside U.S.A.* by Daniel F. Bradley, production manager of Harper's at the time, and now a vice-president of the company, which appeared in *Publishers' Weekly* on July 5, 1947. Most writers do not, I think, appreciate sufficiently the problems their books may present to publishers, and what Mr. Bradley has to say about technical elements in the publication of a long book produced in a hurry is revealing:

> Tinker to Evers to Chance was a happy example of speed and co-operation in the days of the old Chicago Cubs; and "Gunther to Haddon to Harper" was an equally smooth combination that functioned during the production of *Inside U.S.A.* As soon as the first tentative manufacturing and publishing schedule for the book was drawn up, everybody realized that it was going to be a terrific push, and would require the utmost in co-operation and speedy handling if we were going to get the book out anywhere near the

date we set. Just how much would be required, no one really knew, neither the author, the publisher, nor the manufacturer.

The first schedule was soon discarded, and so were the second, third and fourth, and then we simply decided to rush everything. The original plan was that the book would run to about 640 pages, but about Christmastime a recapitulation of copy that had gone through and an estimate of what was to come showed that it would run about 960.

The first hundred pages of copy went to the Haddon Craftsmen, in Scranton, Pa., on October 4 [1946], and the last and 26th batch of copy (2,730 sheets in all) went on March 11 [1947]. Galleys came in in 29 batches starting on October 10 and finishing on March 13. Many of these lots of copy were single chapters, and after the usual copy editing they were sent off to Haddon the same day they were received, so that we had proofs within two days.

At the same time he was writing the book Gunther was reading galleys on what had been set, going over copy with the libel lawyers, and arguing with his experts. Page makeup was delayed because the copy was written by chapters but not in sequence, and when we did finally start makeup, it was necessary to do it without running heads and folios; then as chapters fell into place, revised and folioed pages came in. This made for considerable confusion in handling proofs, both in the plant and in our office. A further makeup complication was that because of the political nature of a lot of the text, we had to hold everything open that had been set until after the results of the last election were known, so that if there were any startling upsets, they could be included without involving re-makeup. This lack of sequence in copy also kept us from doing anything much with the index for a long time; it was not until April 1 that the pages of the last chapter came in from Haddon, so that it was a few days after that that the index was completed. It became apparent during February that we were going to exceed 960 pages and would be lucky to hold the book down to 1,024. It was finally necessary to set the bibliography and acknowledgments (with its list of 872 names) and the index with its 5,197 entries, in six point on seven to a larger measure than the text, in order to keep within the 1,024 pages. The last page of text was okayed on April 1, the acknowledgments on April 11, and the index on April 11. When the Book-of-the-Month Club selected *Inside U.S.A.* we had to go back and cast two additional sets of plates on what we had already cast so that the club could run it in three plants, and Haddon also made an extra half set of curved plates, so that they could run the job on flat-bed perfectors and rotaries at the same time.

Our paper suppliers, Perkins and Squier Company, also co-operated to the fullest extent; they not only kept increasing our order as the number of pages in the book jumped up, but when they were faced with furnishing the stock for the B.O.M. books, they supplied that too; 1,052,000 pounds of text stock was used in the combined run. First plates were cast on March 4 and shortly after that the publication date of May 28 was set, which meant books ready to ship no later than May 6. The printing started on March 27 on one rotary press, and as more plates became available the number of presses was increased. Folding began as soon as sheets were delivered, so that as soon as copies of the last forms dropped off the presses, complete books were in sight. Three kinds of black cloth were used to make our 125,000 covers, and to get away from the slow process of label-pasting, as had been done on all the earlier Gunther titles, we stamped the covers in ink and gold to produce the same effect, even though it was more expensive.

Gunther's prodigious effort in writing the book and reading proofs at the same time, and Haddon's production abilities and speed enabled us to start shipping this 125,000 edition of a 1,024 page volume on May 6, seven months and two days after sending out the first 100 pieces of copy.

Thank you, Mr. Bradley.